ROYAL COMMISSION ON THE PRESS

CHAIRMAN: PROFESSOR O R McGREGOR

Periodicals and the Alternative Press

Research Series 6

Presented to Parliament by Command of Her Majesty

July 1977

LONDON

HER MAJESTY'S STATIONERY OFFICE

£1.35 net

Cmnd. 6810–6

ISBN 0 10 168106 2

FOREWORD BY THE CHAIRMAN

1. The Royal Commission on the Press 1974–77 was set up in 1974 with terms of reference:

To inquire into the factors affecting the maintenance of the independence, diversity and editorial standards of newspapers and periodicals, and the public's freedom of choice of newspapers and periodicals, nationally, regionally and locally, with particular reference to:

(a) the economics of newspaper and periodical publishing distribution;

(b) the interaction of newspaper and periodical interests held by the companies concerned with their other interests and holdings, within and outside the communications industry;

(c) management and labour practices and relations in the newspaper and periodical industry;

(d) conditions and security of employment in the newspaper and periodical industry;

(e) the distribution and concentration of ownership of the newspaper and periodical industry, and the adequacy of existing law in relation thereto;

(f) the responsibilities, constitution and functioning of the Press Council;

and to make recommendations.

2. The Final Report of the Royal Commission was published in July 1977 and this volume forms part of the accompanying Research Series. It presents the research carried out by members of our own Secretariat into periodicals and the alternative press. In so far as previous Royal Commissions considered periodicals, they concentrated on the 'journals of opinion' which deal with politics and current affairs. We have broadened the field of inquiry to include general and leisure magazines, trade, technical and professional publications, as well as those publications which fall outside the world of conventional publishing and are commonly described as the 'alternative' press. In addition, we commissioned a separate study of the women's periodical press which will be published as one of our Working Papers.*

3. The present volume is in two parts. The first describes the periodical press and shows the range of titles, their circulation and readership, and their ownership. We also summarise the finances of periodicals and examine ease of entry into the industry. Many of the data used were provided by the International Publishing Corporation (IPC). We are indebted to them for their permission to publish these data and for the considerable help which they have given to us throughout the preparation of this study and in many other ways.

4. The second part records the findings of the sample survey which we undertook into the alternative press. It casts light on the scope of the alternative press, the opportunities for starting such papers and the problems which their

---

*Dr Cynthia L White, *The Women's Periodical Press in Britain 1946-1974*, Royal Commission on the Press 1974-77, Working Paper Number 4, HMSO, 1977.

publishers need to overcome if they are to succeed. I believe that this study is valuable in drawing attention to the contribution which the alternative press makes to the diversity of subject matter and ideas within the press as a whole and for demonstrating that there is no opinion however bizarre which cannot easily be advanced in print in Britain. We are grateful to all the respondents to the survey and to John Noyce whose *Directory of Alternative Publications* has been very useful to us. I thank particularly Paul Starkey and David Worskett, the members of our Secretariat who carried out the survey.

O R McGregor
July 1977

Part I
The Periodical Press

Contents

List of Tables

CHAPTER 1   RANGE OF TITLES AND TRENDS IN CIRCULATION AND READERSHIP

Introduction

1. The periodical publishing industry is the most diverse section of the press. Its products range from small circulation academic journals to mass circulation women's weekly magazines, and from magazines for particular trades or professions to the popular general interest magazines with circulations of over two million a week.

2. The Shorter Oxford English Dictionary defines a periodical as a magazine "published at regular intervals longer than a day, as monthly . . .". In fact, most periodicals are produced weekly, monthly, or quarterly. This study excludes periodicals which are published annually. It also excludes the 'house magazines' which are published by various organisations, 'part works'[1] and the weekend colour magazines of the national newspapers. Free and controlled circulation magazines are included.

Types of periodical

3. Periodicals are generally classified into two broad groups—general and leisure interest magazines, or to use the trade term 'consumer' magazines, and trade, technical and professional journals—and then into many sub-categories. In evidence to the Royal Commission, the Periodical Publishers Association (PPA) suggested that "the essential difference between technical journals and other periodicals is that they are as much a part of the industry, trade or profession they serve as they are part of the press, and the role of the technical press is to provide news and information, to educate and to advise".

Number of titles

4. It is not possible to state with certainty the total number of periodicals, as each of the trade directories gives a different total. For example, the *Newspaper Press Directory* gave a total of 4,438 'general and specialist periodicals' in 1974, whereas the *Willing's Press Guide* gave a total of 4,718 periodicals, and 3,379 titles were listed in *British Rate and Data* (BRAD) (October edition).

5. Table 1 shows the number of periodicals listed in the *Newspaper Press Directory* in selected years between 1948 and 1976. These figures include magazines published in the Republic of Ireland, where there were about 120 titles in each year.

TABLE 1
NUMBER OF PERIODICAL TITLES, 1948–1976

Number of titles									Net change	
1948	*1951*	*1961*	*1966*	*1970*	*1971*	*1974*	*1975*	*1976*	*1961– 1971*	*1971– 1976*
3,715	3,346	3,851	4,068	4,258	4,461	4,438	4,556	4,319	+610	−142

Source: *Newspaper Press Directory*.

[1] 'Part works' are publications which are issued regularly over a period of years, which when accumulated form a complete set. They were most popular in the late 1960s. It has been estimated that, in 1969, 33 separate part works were on the bookstalls at the same time.

6. There was a net increase of 610 in the number of titles between 1961 and 1971, but a net decrease of 142 between 1971 and 1976. The total number of titles in 1976 is, however, almost a thousand more than in 1951. The size of the annual change in the total number of titles has varied considerably over the period 1961 to 1976. The largest increase was recorded between 1970 and 1971, and the largest fall between 1975 and 1976. In general, there appear to have been greater changes in the latter part of the period 1961 to 1976. This suggests that the periodical industry may have become more sensitive to changes in the general economic climate, possibly because it has become increasingly specialised and segmented.

Range of titles

7. The categories of periodical used in the *Newspaper Press Directory* (NPD) and in *British Rate and Data* (BRAD) are useful as a means of demonstrating the range of subjects covered by the periodical press. Table 2 shows the main categories used in these directories in 1974, and the numbers of titles in them. Only BRAD includes separate listings of general and leisure interest ('consumer') magazines, and of trade, technical and professional journals. Of the 3,379 periodicals listed in the October 1974 edition of BRAD, 34% were 'consumer' magazines and 66% trade, technical and professional. The 'consumer' magazines were divided into 47 categories and the trade, technical and professional journals into 97 categories. The listings in BRAD suggest that almost one-third of all periodicals were contained in the ten major categories in Table 2.

TABLE 2

MAJOR CATEGORIES OF PERIODICAL, 1974

Newspaper Press Directory		*British Rate and Data*	
Category	Number of titles	Category	Number of titles
Medical...	280	Medical*	175
Sciences	196	Sciences*	140
Engineering	195	Education*	110
Education	194	Business, finance	68
Societies and organisations ...	191	Agriculture and farming* ...	90
Sports and recreations ...	154	Sporting	83
Agriculture	153	Women's interest	75
Women's	116	Armed services*	73
Politics and current affairs ...	114	Politics and current affairs ...	68
Building trade	104	Music, antiques and arts ...	66

Source: Royal Commission on the Press 1974–1977, from *Newspaper Press Directory* and *British Rate and Data*.

Note: * classed as trade, technical and professional journals.

8. A different picture of the relative importance of the various areas of interest covered by periodical publishing emerges if the size of circulation is taken into account, but this comparison is limited because there are audited or published circulation figures for only about one-third of both 'consumer' and trade and technical publications. Nevertheless, the figures which are available show, despite the fact that trade, technical and professional publications outnumber 'consumer' magazines by about two to one, that there are only 12 trade, technical and professional publications with known circulations of over 100,000 as against 37 'consumer' magazines. The eight largest BRAD categories of 'consumer' magazine ranked by size of circulation in 1974 are shown in Table 3; only one of these (women's interests) is among the largest five categories in terms of number of titles. Similarly, only agriculture and farming among the BRAD trade, technical and professional categories contains both a journal with a circulation of over 100,000 and a large number of titles.[1]

TABLE 3

EIGHT MAJOR CATEGORIES OF 'CONSUMER' MAGAZINE, AND THE NUMBER OF THESE MAGAZINES WITH SPECIFIED CIRCULATIONS, 1974

Category	Circulation (thousands)							Total number of titles
	Not available	50 or less	51–100	101–150	151–200	201–250	Over 250	
Children's comics ...	6	1	2	10	6	3	4	32
General interest	13	6	9	1	—	—	6	35
Home interest	9	1	2	—	2	1	2	17
Sex magazines	3	2	1	3	1	—	5	15
Motoring, etc.	28	3	7	8	3	—	1	50
TV and Radio	3	1	1	—	—	—	2	7
Teenage and pop... ...	8	1	1	3	3	4	3	23
Women's magazines ...	23	3	10	12	8	6	13	75
Sub-Total...	93	18	33	37	23	14	36	254
All others...	689	143	42	18	7	1	1	901
Total	782	161	75	55	30	15	37	1,155

Source: Royal Commission on the Press 1974–77, from *British Rate and Data*.

[1] Table 18 shows the size distribution of the largest categories of trade, technical and professional publications.

Categories of 'consumer' magazine

9. The relative importance of the various categories of 'consumer' magazine can also be seen from Table 4. It is based on data supplied by IPC and follows its method of classification to show trends in the total number of copies sold annually in five 'consumer' magazine sectors over the period 1965 to 1975. These sectors, each of which roughly corresponds to a very broad market for readers, are themselves amalgamations of the 53 categories used by IPC. Table 5 shows the numbers of copies sold and consumers' expenditure[1] in the most important of these categories in 1975. These figures cover only those titles for which circulation data are available.[2] Table 6 gives the number of such titles in each sector from 1965 to 1975.

TABLE 4

GROSS ANNUAL CIRCULATION[a] OF 'CONSUMER' MAGAZINES BY SECTOR, 1965–1975

millions

Sector	1965	1970	1971	1972	1973	1974	1975
General interest ...	985	935	903	939	975	939	871
Adult women's ...	560	493	478	487	487	487	457
Young women's ...	47	77	77	78	74	67	65
Teenage	87	84	77	97	178	103	80
Children's	482	518	501	479	446	367	329
Total... ...	2,160	2,108	2,036	2,080	2,160	1,964	1,802

Source: IPC.

Note:

(a) Gross annual circulation equals the total number of copies sold in a year.

---

(1) 'Consumers' expenditure' is the amount spent on periodicals by their purchasers.

(2) Children's titles are also included but circulation data are not usually available for them because these are of most interest to advertisers and children's magazines carry little advertising. The magazines which do not have audited circulations are estimated to account for less than 10% of the estimated total circulation of magazines with and without circulation data.

TABLE 5

TOTAL NUMBER OF COPIES OF 'CONSUMER' MAGAZINES SOLD(a) AND CONSUMERS' EXPENDITURE IN 1975, BY SECTOR

Sector	Copies sold per annum		Consumers' expenditure	
	millions	%	£ million	%
Adult women's				
Women's weeklies	393·1	21·8	32·4	16·6
General	37·7	2·1	7·3	3·7
Feminine interest	10·7	0·6	3·3	1·7
Home interest	15·2	0·8	3·6	1·8
Total	456·6	25·3	46·7	24·0
Young women's				
General	19·3	1·1	5·3	2·7
Romantic fiction	45·8	2·5	2·6	1·3
Total	65·0	3·6	7·9	4·1
Teenage				
General	77·0	4·3	5·3	2·7
Pop	3·0	0·2	0·5	0·3
Total	80·0	4·4	5·9	3·0
Children's				
Nursery comics	38·8	2·2	2·9	1·5
Humorous	109·8	6·1	5·9	3·0
Boys' adventure	91·1	5·1	5·2	2·7
Soccer comics	12·4	0·7	1·4	0·7
Girls' adventure	59·1	3·3	3·1	1·6
Educational comics	7·1	0·4	1·0	0·5
Junior TV guides	11·0	0·6	0·8	0·4
Total	329·4	18·3	19·9	10·2
General interest				
Home entertainment guides ...	357·2	19·8	32·8	16·8
Popular magazines ...	190·9	10·6	17·0	8·7
Politics and current affairs ...	28·5	1·6	8·4	4·3
Sex	27·6	1·5	13·3	6·8
Pop music	31·2	1·7	3·7	1·9
Gardening	24·0	1·3	2·6	1·3
Classified advertising ...	24·0	1·3	2·3	1·2
General motoring	19·7	1·1	3·7	1·9
Motorcycling	18·1	1·0	2·6	1·3
Enthusiast motoring	7·5	0·4	2·0	1·0
Religion and mysticism	25·7	1·4	1·9	1·0
Other 27 categories	96·1	6·6	24·0	12·3
Total	870·5	48·3	114·4	58·8
Grand Total	1,801·5	100·0	194·7	100·0

Source: IPC.

Note:

(a) Includes all titles for which circulation data are available on a reasonably regular basis and estimates of circulations of children's titles.

5

TABLE 6

NUMBER OF 'CONSUMER' MAGAZINES(a) BY SECTOR, 1965–1975

Sector	Number of titles		
	1965	1970	1975
Adult women's			
Women's weeklies	9	9	11
General	6	7	8
Feminine interest	13	16	13
Home interest	7	5	9
Total...	35	37	41
Young women's			
General	1	3	5
Romantic fiction	10	14	14
Total...	11	17	19
Teenage			
General	7	7	6
Pop	—	—	3
Total...	7	7	9
Children's			
Nursery comics	7	10	9
Humorous	8	8	13
Boys' adventure	12	12	15
Soccer comics	—	5	1
Girls' adventure	4	5	7
Educational comics...	5	4	2
Junior TV guides	—	—	1
Total...	36	44	48
General interest			
Politics and current affairs ...	7	10	14
Religion and mysticism	17	17	15
Sex	3	9	10
General motoring	12	13	12
Other...	154	169	168
Total...	193	218	237
Grand Total	282	323	354

Source: IPC.

Note:

(a) Includes all titles for which circulation data are available on a reasonably regular basis and children's titles for which circulation data are not available.

Trends in circulation and readership of 'consumer' magazines

10. Table 4 shows that the gross annual circulation of all 'consumer' magazines has fallen by about 1,300 million since 1965. Only young women's titles had a gross annual circulation greater in 1975 than in 1965, but even in this case the 1975 circulation was 13 million less than in the peak year of 1972. Children's titles had decreased considerably in gross annual circulation by 1975, despite a slight increase between 1965 and the early 1970s. In the following paragraphs, the major sectors of general and leisure interest ('consumer') magazines are examined in more detail.

Adult women's titles

11. IPC divides women's magazines into two sectors: adult women's titles and young women's titles. There is probably a considerable overlap between the readership of these two, just as there is between young women's and teenage titles.

12. Table 5 shows that, apart from the omnibus general interest sector, adult women's magazines form the largest sector of 'consumer' magazines, in terms both of copies sold and consumers' expenditure. The number of adult women's magazines for which circulation data are available has increased by six since 1965, a net increase of four coming after 1970. The adult women's market is dominated by the women's weeklies which include the six mass circulation magazines, *Woman, Woman's Own, Woman's Realm, Woman's Weekly* (all published by IPC), and *My Weekly* and *People's Friend* (both published by D C Thomson). However, as can be seen from Table 7, the circulation of these women's weeklies has fallen considerably since 1961. Then, IPC owned the largest five women's weeklies; one has since ceased publication (*Woman's Mirror* in 1967) and, by 1976, D C Thomson's *My Weekly* had overtaken the smallest circulation IPC women's weekly, *Woman's Realm*.

TABLE 7

MAJOR ADULT WOMEN'S WEEKLY MAGAZINES, CIRCULATION 1961, 1971 AND 1976

Title	Publisher	Circulation[a] (thousands)				
		1961	% change	1971	% change	1976
Woman	IPC	2,969	−32·2	2,013	−23·9	1,532
Woman's Own ...	IPC	2,161	−22·4	1,676	− 8·2	1,539
Woman's Weekly ...	IPC	1,420	+21·1	1,719	− 4·3	1,645
Woman's Realm ...	IPC	1,300	−24·2	986	−19·1	798
Woman's Mirror[b]	IPC	1,153	—	—	—	—
My Weekly ...	D C Thomson ...	130[c]	+543·1	836	+ 5·6	883
People's Friend ...	D C Thomson ...	419	+33·4	559	+29·9	726

Source: Royal Commission on the Press 1974–77, from *British Rate and Data.*

Notes:

(a) Average weekly circulation for the period January–June of each year.

(b) Merged with *Woman* in 1967.

(c) Estimated.

13. The other categories of adult women's magazines consist mainly of monthlies. They include general titles, such as *She, Cosmopolitan, Annabel, Living* and *Family Circle*, which account for nearly three times as many copies sold as the other two categories, feminine and home interest. The feminine

TABLE 8

SELECTED WOMEN'S MONTHLY MAGAZINES, CIRCULATION 1961, 1971 AND 1976

Title	Publisher	Circulation(a) (thousands)				
		1961	% change	1971	% change	1976
General interest						
Woman's Journal	IPC	255	−35·7	164	−11·6	145
Everywoman(b) ...	IPC	273	—	—	—	—
She	National Magazine Company ...	251	+17·9	296	− 2·0	290
Cosmopolitan(c) ...	National Magazine Company ...	—	—	—	—	379
Annabel(d) ...	D C Thomson ...	—	—	149	+33·6	199
Family Circle(e) ...	Thomson Publications ...	—	—	1,203	−30·1	841
Living(f)	Thomson Publications ...	—	—	575	+ 5·6	607
Feminine interest						
Stitchcraft ...	The Condé Nast Publications ...	125	+12·0	140	−40·7	83
Vogue	The Condé Nast Publications ...	165	−32·7	111	+ 4·5	116
Flair(g)	IPC	148	−32·4	100	—	—
Mother	IPC	81	+27·1	103	−21·4	81
Woman and Home	IPC	696	+ 2·3	712	− 9·1	647
Sewing and Knitting(h) ...	IPC	—	—	181	−41·4	106
Over 21(j) ...	MS Publications ...	—	—	98	+21·4	119
Home and Family	The Mother's Union	398	−35·7	256	−44·1	143
Harpers & Queen(k)	National Magazine Company ...	55	+14·5	63	+ 4·8	66
Pins and Needles	Thomson Publications ...	121	+44·6	175	−47·4	92
Home interest						
House & Garden	The Condé Nast Publications ...	50	+74·0	87	+34·5	117
Homemaker ...	IPC	224	−43·3	127	−11·1	113
Homes and Gardens	IPC	185	+ 3·2	191	− 6·8	178
Ideal Home ...	IPC	215	−24·7	162	+16·7	189
Good Housekeeping	National Magazine Company ...	185	+ 1·6	188	+53·7	289
Womancraft(l) ...	National Magazine Company ...	—	—	—	—	89

Source: Royal Commission on the Press 1974–77, from *British Rate and Data*.

Notes:

(a) Average monthly circulation for the period January–June of each year.

(b) Merged with *Woman and Home* in 1967.

(c) Launched 1972.

(d) Launched 1966.

(e) Launched 1964.

(f) Launched 1967.

(g) Merged with *Woman's Journal* in 1972.

(h) Launched 1966.

(j) Launched 1971.

(k) *Harpers & Queen* was first published in 1971 when the former *Harpers Bazaar* and *The Queen* were merged. The 1961 circulation shown is for *Harpers Bazaar*.

(l) Launched 1972.

interest category includes *Harpers and Queen, Vogue, Over 21*, and home interest takes in *Good Housekeeping, Ideal Home* and *Homes and Gardens*. Table 8 shows the mixed fortunes of women's monthly magazines since 1961. Two magazines launched since then, *Family Circle* and *Living*, have achieved circulations of over 500,000. But other titles have lost sales. It is, however, not possible to detect a general trend in circulation from this table because a large number of women's monthly magazines do not have recorded circulations.

Young women's titles

14. Young women's titles account for only about one-twentieth of total audited copy sales. This is the smallest 'consumer' periodical sector used by IPC, although it is larger than all but two of the general interest categories. The titles can be divided into general magazines, like *Honey* and *19*, and romantic fiction magazines, like *True with My Love* and *Loving*. Table 9 shows the circulation of some of these magazines in 1961, 1971 and 1976.

TABLE 9
SELECTED YOUNG WOMEN'S MAGAZINES, CIRCULATION 1961, 1971 AND 1976

Title	Publisher	Circulation(a) (thousands)				
		1961	% change	1971	% change	1976
General interest						
Honey (M) ...	IPC	104	+71·2	178	− 3·9	171
19(b) (M) ...	IPC	—	—	201	−18·4	164
Look Now(c)(M)...	IPC	—	—	—	—	188
Romantic Fiction						
True Story (M) ...	Argus Press Holdings	} 358	+19·8	} 429	−30·1	} 300
True Romances (M)	Argus Press Holdings					
Woman's Story (M)	Argus Press Holdings	NR	—	107	−33·6	71
Hers(d) (M) ...	IPC	—	—	191	−23·6	146
True Magazine(e) (M)	IPC	194	+11·3	216	−16·2	181
Marilyn(f) (W) ...	IPC	229	—	—	—	—
Roxy(g) (W) ...	IPC	215	—	—	—	—
Loving(h)(W) ...	IPC	—	—	236	−25·4	176
Love Affair(j) (W)	IPC	—	—	250	−47·2	132
Red Letter (W) ...	D C Thomson ...	175*	−17·3	144	−38·9	88
Red Star Weekly	D C Thomson ...	123*	−19·5	99	−29·3	70
Secrets (W) ...	D C Thomson ...	142*	− 1·4	140	−37·9	87
Story World(k) (W)	D C Thomson ...	—	—	—	—	98

Source: Royal Commission on the Press 1974–77 from *British Rate and Data*.
Notes:
   * Estimate.
   M = Monthly.
   W = Weekly.
   NR = Not recorded.
   (a) Average weekly or monthly circulation for the period January–June of each year.
   (b) Launched 1968.
   (c) Launched 1972.
   (d) Launched 1966.
   (e) Now re-titled *True with My Love*.
   (f) Ceased publication.
   (g) Ceased publication.
   (h) Launched 1970.
   (j) Launched 1971. Circulation for 1971 is the initial print order.
   (k) Launched 1974.

Teenage and children's magazines

15. Young teenage titles consist of general magazines like *Jackie* and *Diana*, and pop publications, like *Fab 208* and *Osmonds' World*. This market experiences a relatively large number of births and deaths.[1] The average life expectancy of a title is short: few live longer than ten years and new magazines generally have a planned life of five years or less.

16. Within the children's sector, humorous comics such as *Dandy*, *Beano*, *Beezer* and *Topper* are estimated to be the largest category in terms of copies sold, with boys' magazines such as *The Victor* and *Hotspur* not far behind; educational comics for children are the smallest category in this sector. There is some distinction between magazines for boys and for girls, but this is less so with the comics for younger children. This market, too, is characterised by a high proportion of births and deaths.

17. Table 10 shows selected teenage and children's publications and their circulations in 1971 and 1976. Judged by this selection there has been a marked fall in sales since 1971. But the table cannot be taken to be representative since it excludes several well-known titles for which circulation data are not available.

TABLE 10

SELECTED[a] TEENAGE AND CHILDREN'S PUBLICATIONS, CIRCULATION 1971 AND 1976

Title	Publisher	Launch date	Circulation[b] (thousands)		
			1971	% change	1976
Teenage					
Fab 208	IPC	1964	128	− 8·6	117
Mates	IPC	1975	—	—	177
Mirabelle	IPC	1956	181	−57·5	77
Pink	IPC	1973	—	—	171
Jackie	D C Thomson	1964	626	− 3·4	605
Children's					
Jack and Jill	IPC	1954	160	—	NR
Look and Learn ...	IPC	1962	127	—	NR
Look-in	IPC	1971	277	−32·1	188
Whizzer and Chips ...	IPC	1969	220	—	NR
Pippin in Playland ...	Polystyle Publications ...	1966	205	−50·7	101
Bunty	D C Thomson	1958	466	−57·3	199
Hotspur	D C Thomson	1933	209	−35·9	134
Judy	D C Thomson	1960	314	−64·3	112
The Victor	D C Thomson	1961	340	−42·6	195

Source: Royal Commission on the Press 1974–77 from *British Rate and Data*.

Notes:

NR = Not recorded.

(a) The selection is one of publications with circulation data. Several well-known comics, such as *Dandy*, *Beano*, *Beezer* do not have recorded circulations.

(b) Average weekly circulation for the period January–June of each year.

[1] See further Chapter 4.

General and special interest magazines

18. The general interest sector, which is twice the size of the next largest sector (adult women's), is an amalgamation of 38 general and special interest categories ranging from home entertainment guides like *Radio Times* and *TV Times* and such popular general interest titles as *Titbits, Weekend, Reveille, Weekly News, Reader's Digest,* to more specialised interests such as motoring, angling, woodworking and gardening. It also includes sex magazines and journals of political and current affairs, both of which are examined separately in this section. Thus, the range and diversity of magazines in this sector is immense.

19. The two largest categories in terms of circulation are the home entertainment guides and the popular general interest titles. As Table 11 shows, the latter have declined substantially in circulation since 1961. Programme

TABLE 11

SELECTED GENERAL AND SPECIAL INTEREST MAGAZINES, CIRCULATION 1961, 1971 AND 1976

Title	Publisher	Circulation[a] (thousands)				
		1961	% change	1971	% change	1976
Programme magazines						
Radio Times ...	BBC Publications ...	6,146	−45·0	3,378	+ 3·3	3,490
TV Times ...	ITV Publications ...	3,778	−17·2	3,129	+ 5·8	3,310
Popular magazines						
Weekend	Associated Newspapers Group	1,239	− 2·3	1,211	−34·6	792
Titbits	IPC	764	−13·6	660	−31·5	452
Reveille	Mirror Group Newspapers[b] ...	1,716	−46·0	926	−40·4	552
Reader's Digest ...	Reader's Digest Association ...	1,238	+21·2	1,501	− 1·3	1,481
Weekly News ...	D C Thomson ...	NR	—	1,394	− 3·4	1,346
Special interest						
Angling Times ...	EMAP National Publications ...	137	+ 6·6	146	+ 6·2	155
Garden News ...	EMAP National Publications ...	42	+102·4	85	+84·7	157
Motor Cycle News	EMAP National Publications ...	67	+55·2	104	+84·6	192
Autocar	IPC	141[c]	−29·1	100[d]	−29·0	71
Popular Gardening	IPC	180	− 6·1	169	− 7·1	157
Practical Householder ...	IPC	373	−48·8	191	−29·8	134
Practical Motorist	IPC	244	−34·4	160	−27·5	116
Do-It-Yourself ...	Link House Publications ...	284	−41·9	165	−34·5	108

Source: Royal Commission on the Press 1974–77 from *British Rate and Data.*

Notes:
(a) Average weekly or monthly circulation for the period January–June for each year.
(b) Mirror Group Newspapers and IPC are subsidiaries of Reed International.
(c) January–December 1960.
(d) January–December 1970.

guides, more especially the *Radio Times*, also suffered a large fall in circulation between 1961 and 1971 but there has been a modest increase in sales since then. One of the major reasons for the fall was the expansion of television coverage by newspapers. Table 11 shows that, by contrast, some of the more specialised magazines, in particular those devoted to motor cycles and gardening, have shown a considerable increase in circulation since 1961.

20. Sex magazines have increased both in number and in circulation since 1965. Table 12 shows that, of the current large circulation titles, only two, *Men Only* and *Playboy*, were in existence in 1961, but the former was published by another company and was very different from today's magazine. There are now seven major magazines of this sort, as well as a much larger number of smaller titles. The circulations of three magazines for which figures are available have more than doubled since 1961.

TABLE 12

SELECTED SEX MAGAZINES, CIRCULATION 1961, 1971 AND 1976

Title	Publisher	Launch date	Circulation[a] (thousands)		
			1971	% change	1976
Mayfair	Fisk Publishing Company ...	1966	164	+144·5	401
Fiesta	Galaxy Publications	1966	NR	—	234
Playboy	H M Hefner	1954	90	− 30·0	63
Penthouse	Penthouse Publications ...	1964	218	+ 96·8	429[b]
Men Only[c] ...	Paul Raymond Publications	1935	150	+189·3	434
Club International...	Paul Raymond Publications	1972	—	—	324

Source: Royal Commission on the Press 1974–77 from *British Rate and Data*.

Notes:
NR = Not recorded.
   (*a*) Average monthly circulation for the period January–June of each year.
   (*b*) January–June 1975.
   (*c*) Formerly owned by IPC.

21. The Royal Commission 1961–62 identified seven journals of opinion, but of these only *The Economist*, the *New Statesman*, *Spectator* and *Tribune* remain. (*Time and Tide* still exists but in a different form.) However, new magazines have been launched with, in part at least, comparable content; for example, *New Society* was started in 1962 by Harrison-Raison (it is now owned by IPC), and the Labour Party now publish their own *Labour Weekly*. Indeed, we estimate that at least 200 periodicals, many of them alternative publications, are now devoted partly to the interpretation of politics and society. Table 13 shows that the circulation of the established journals of opinion has fallen since 1961, with the notable exception of *The Economist* the circulation of which has risen from some 65,000 in 1961 to 133,000 in 1967.

TABLE 13

SELECTED JOURNALS OF OPINION, CIRCULATION 1961, 1971 AND 1976

Title	Publisher	Circulation[a] (thousands)				
		1961	% change	1971	% change	1976
The Listener ...	BBC Publications ...	98	−52·1	47	−19·1	38
The Economist ...	The Economist Newspaper Limited	65	+58·5	103	+29·1	133
Encounter[b] ...	Encounter Limited	26	−19·2	21	− 9·5	19
New Society[c] ...	IPC	—	—	36	−11·1	32
Labour Weekly[d] ...	The Labour Party...	—	—	NR	—	21
Spectator	The Spectator Limited	48	—	NR	—	13
New Statesman ...	Statesman and Nation Publishing Company ...	85	−11·6	76	−43·4	43

Source: Royal Commission on the Press 1974–77 from *British Rate and Data.*

Notes:

NR = Not recorded.

(a) Average weekly or monthly circulation for the period January–June of each year.

(b) Monthly.

(c) Launched in 1962 by Harrison-Raison.

(d) Launched in 1971. Circulation is for the period January–June 1975.

Readership of 'consumer' magazines

22. The *National Readership Survey* (NRS)[1] collects details of the numbers and types of reader of a selection of 'consumer' magazines. It presents analyses of the readership both of individual magazines and of groups of these magazines defined by their content and frequency of publication. In 1976, over half the adult population read[2] at least one of the general weekly magazines included in the NRS, and over one-third at least one of the general monthly magazines. Some 56% of adult women read one or more of the women's weeklies included in the NRS, and 47% one or more of the women's monthlies; just over one-third of all adults read at least one of either group of women's magazines. In contrast, over 70% of the adult population read a national daily newspaper and over 80% a national Sunday. However, because only a selection of magazine titles are included in the NRS, the full extent of magazine readership is not known.

23. Tables 14 and 15 show readership penetration in 1976, by sex, age and social grade, of some of the women's magazines and of some of the general and special interest magazines included in the *National Readership Survey.* The

---

(1) Published by the Joint Industry Committee for National Readership Surveys (JICNARS).

(2) Readership is 'average issue readership' and represents the number of people who claim to have read or looked at one or more copies of a given publication during a period equal to the interval at which the publication appears.

TABLE 14

READERSHIP PENETRATION OF SELECTED WOMEN'S MAGAZINES BY SEX, AGE AND SOCIAL GRADE, 1976

Percentages of total population(a)

Title	Total	By Sex		By Age (Women only)						By Social Grade (Women only)					
		Men	Women	15–24	25–34	35–44	45–54	55–64	65+	A	B	C₁	C₂	D	E
Women's weeklies															
Woman	16	6	26	34	28	27	28	24	19	24	26	30	29	24	17
Woman's Own ...	17	7	27	33	29	28	28	25	20	20	26	30	29	27	18
Woman's Weekly ...	12	4	20	15	17	20	22	24	21	10	17	22	21	18	20
Woman's Realm ...	9	3	15	12	13	17	18	17	15	7	13	16	17	14	13
My Weekly ...	8	2	13	9	12	11	14	15	15	3	7	12	14	13	16
People's Friend ...	6	2	10	4	7	9	11	14	16	3	5	10	10	10	16
Women's Monthlies															
Annabel	2	1	3	5	3	4	4	3	2	4	4	4	3	3	2
Family Circle ...	9	4	13	13	20	19	14	12	5	19	20	17	14	9	5
Good Housekeeping ...	6	2	9	9	11	11	10	11	5	24	21	13	7	5	3
She	5	3	7	10	9	9	8	5	2	12	13	10	6	4	2
Woman and Home ...	8	2	13	10	13	14	16	16	10	19	21	17	12	9	7
Young Women's															
Honey	2	*	3	10	2	2	2	2	*	7	4	5	2	2	*
19	2	3	3	15	2	1	1	1	*	7	4	5	3	3	*

Source: *National Readership Survey 1976.*

Notes:
* Less than 0·5%.
(a) Aged 15+.

14

TABLE 15

READERSHIP PENETRATION OF SELECTED GENERAL AND SPECIAL INTEREST MAGAZINES BY SEX, AGE AND SOCIAL GRADE, 1976

Percentages of all adults(a)

Title	Total	By Sex		By Age						By Social Grade					
		Men	Women	15–24	25–34	35–44	45–54	55–64	65+	A	B	C₁	C₂	D	E
Programme magazines															
Radio Times	23	22	24	26	23	24	22	22	20	43	35	28	20	18	17
TV Times	24	22	25	28	25	25	23	22	19	24	25	25	23	23	20
Popular Magazines															
Reader's Digest ...	18	20	16	18	20	21	20	18	12	24	25	23	18	13	8
Reveille	6	6	6	6	6	7	8	6	4	1	2	5	8	8	4
Titbits	5	6	5	7	6	4	6	4	2	1	2	4	7	7	3
Weekend	8	9	8	12	11	8	8	7	4	2	3	8	10	10	6
Weekly News	10	9	11	9	9	9	11	11	10	*	3	7	11	14	11
Sex magazines															
Mayfair	4	7	1	6	8	4	3	1	*	4	3	4	5	4	1
Specialist magazines															
Do-It-Yourself ...	4	6	3	4	6	6	5	4	2	4	4	5	5	3	1
Practical Householder	3	5	2	2	5	5	4	3	1	2	4	4	4	2	1
Practical Motorist ...	3	6	1	4	4	4	4	3	1	1	2	4	5	3	*

Source: *National Readership Survey*, 1976.

Notes:

* Less than 0·5%.

(a) Aged 15+.

tables suggest that these women's monthlies are more 'up-market' and, apart from *Woman and Home*, have a somewhat younger age profile than most of the women's weeklies. However, the two most widely read women's weeklies, *Woman* and *Woman's Own*, have a greater readership penetration among women under 45 than among those over. A significant proportion of men read women's magazines. Readership penetration of the general and special interest magazines included in Table 15 is, in general, greater for men than for women, the exceptions being the *Weekly News* and the two programme magazines. Apart from the *Weekly News*, these magazines tend to be read more widely among the younger age groups and, excepting the programme magazines and the *Reader's Digest*, in social grades C and D.

Changes in readership[1]

24. Table 16 shows changes in readership, readership penetration and women readers per copy of women's magazines between 1971 and 1976. All but two of the women's weeklies have lost sales since 1971 (see Table 7) but, as Table 16 shows, there has been a marked increase in women readers per copy so that the loss of readers is proportionately less than that of sales. The opposite seems to have happened with some of the women's monthly and young women's magazines: readership penetration and readers per copy have fallen since 1971 whilst sales have in some cases gone up or fallen proportionately less than readership (see Tables 8 and 9). As Table 17 shows, this has also happened with several of the general and special interest magazines so that, apparently, more of the readers that remain buy their own copies than was the case in 1971.

---

[1] This section is based upon readership figures taken from the *National Readership Survey* 1971 and 1976. The percentage changes shown are the Royal Commission's own calculations. The confidence limits of the Survey data have not been calculated and the percentage changes shown should be regarded as only approximate. The confidence limits of the Survey data are discussed in Appendix F of the *National Readership Survey*, 1976.

TABLE 16

SELECTED WOMEN'S MAGAZINES, CHANGES IN WOMEN'S(a) READERSHIP, 1971–1976

Title	Average issue readership			Readership penetration(b)			Number of readers per copy		
	1971 (thousands)	1976 (thousands)	% change 1971–1976	1971 %	1976 %	% change 1971–1976	1971	1976	% change 1971–1976
Women's weeklies									
Woman	6,423	5,725	−11	29·8	26·4	−11	3·2	3·9	+22
Woman's Own ...	5,722	5,825	+2	26·5	26·9	+2	3·5	3·9	+11
Woman's Weekly...	3,926	4,256	+8	18·2	19·7	+8	2·3	3·0	+30
Woman's Realm ...	3,701	3,239	−12	17·2	14·9	−13	3·7	4·2	+14
My Weekly ...	2,578	2,767	+7	11·9	12·8	+8	n.a.	n.a.	—
People's Friend ...	1,480	2,196	+48	6·9	10·1	+46	n.a.	n.a.	—
Women's monthlies									
Annabel	754	713	−5	3·5	3·3	−6	n.a.	n.a.	—
Family Circle ...	3,400	2,851	−16	15·8	13·1	−17	n.a.	3·4	—
Good Housekeeping	2,167	1,972	−9	10·0	9·1	−9	11·2	6·9	−39
She	1,740	1,495	−14	8·1	6·9	−15	5·8	5·1	−12
Woman and Home ...	3,064	2,779	−9	14·2	12·8	−10	4·3	4·6	+7
Young Women's									
Honey	1,112	618	−44	5·2	2·8	−46	6·3	3·7	−31
19	975	721	−26	4·5	3·3	−17	5·0	4·7	−6

Source: Royal Commission on the Press 1974–77, from the *National Readership Survey* 1971 and 1976.

Notes:

n.a. = Not available.

(a) Aged 15+.

(b) Defined as the percentage of all adult women reading the magazine in question.

17

TABLE 17

SELECTED GENERAL AND SPECIAL INTEREST MAGAZINES; CHANGES IN READERSHIP 1971–1976, ALL ADULTS(a)

Title	Average issue readership			Readership penetration(b)			Readers per copy		
	1971 (thousands)	1976 (thousands)	% change 1971–1976	1971 %	1976 %	% change 1971–1976	1971	1976	% change 1971–1976
Programme magazines									
Radio Times	9,549	9,553	*	23·1	23·0	*	2·8	2·7	— 4
TV Times	9,852	9,753	— 1	23·9	23·5	— 2	3·1	2·9	— 7
Popular magazines									
Reader's Digest	9,242	7,431	— 20	22·4	17·9	— 20	n.a.	n.a.	—
Reveille	4,496	2,469	— 45	10·9	5·9	— 46	5·0	4·5	—10
Tibits	2,685	2,065	— 23	6·5	5·0	— 23	4·2	4·9	+17
Weekend	5,323	3,439	— 35	12·9	8·3	— 36	4·5	4·7	+ 4
Weekly News	4,537	4,084	— 10	11·0	9·8	— 11	n.a.	n.a.	—
Sex magazines									
Mayfair	628	1,648	+164	1·5	4·0	+167	3·6	n.a.	—
Specialist magazines									
Do-It-Yourself ...	3,127	1,769	— 43	7·6	4·3	— 43	18·7	16·7	—11
Practical Householder ...	2,445	1,349	— 45	5·9	3·2	— 46	12·7	10·7	—16
Practical Motorist ...	3,300	1,401	— 58	8·0	3·4	— 58	20·9	13·0	—38

Source: Royal Commission on the Press 1974–77, from the *National Readership Survey* 1971 and 1976.

Notes:

* Less than 0·5%.

n.a. = Not available.

(a) Aged 15+.

(b) Defined as the percentage of all adults reading the magazine in question.

Categories of trade, technical and professional journal

25. The distinction between trade, technical and professional journals and 'consumer' magazines is, in some cases, arbitrary. For example, we have classed *The Economist* as part of the 'consumer' section but it is listed in *British Rate and Data* (BRAD) under the trade, technical and professional category of business management. But, in general, the two types of magazine can be distinguished fairly easily.

26. The Periodical Publishers' Association (PPA) suggest[1] that trade, technical and professional publications can themselves be divided into two sorts: 'vertical' journals which cover one industry, trade or profession, and 'horizontal' journals which have a wider readership. It is the 'horizontal' journal which it is sometimes difficult to distinguish from 'consumer' publications. Here, however, the categories listed in BRAD are used. Table 18 shows the largest fifteen categories of trade, technical and professional journals in the October 1974 edition of BRAD, together with the number of titles in each, and the number of known circulations of different sizes.

Circulation of trade, technical and professional journals

27. We have not studied the number of titles or circulations in detail, but there seems to have been a rapid increase in both since 1961. However, circulation data are sparse, partly because the proportion of free or controlled circulation titles is high in some categories, but more generally because many titles do not advertise their circulations. Thus, no aggregate circulation figures are available. Some publications have a high proportion of their sales in overseas markets. The PPA have pointed to the value of these exports in evidence to the Royal Commission:

> The importance of the technical press to the country's exports cannot be over-stressed. [As a result] many British companies receive orders from foreign customers for products advertised in a journal. The dissemination of ideas, processes and methods . . . plays a considerable part in enhancing this country's prestige overseas.

Readership of trade, technical and professional journals

28. No trade, technical or professional publications are included in the *National Readership Survey*. The readership of specialist journals is very high in the industries they serve and which, as the PPA point out, they are in many respects part of.

---

(1) Evidence to the Royal Commission on the Press 1974–77.

TABLE 18

CATEGORIES OF TRADE, TECHNICAL AND PROFESSIONAL PERIODICALS WITH 15 OR MORE TITLES AND THE NUMBER OF THESE PERIODICALS WITH SPECIFIED CIRCULATIONS, 1974

Category	Total number of titles	Circulation (thousands)					
		Not available	Less than 25	26–50	51–75	76–100	Over 100
Accountancy	18	8	5	2	3	—	—
Advertising	23	10	12	1	—	—	—
Aeronautical	22	10	7	4	1	—	—
Agriculture and Farming	89	65	17	4	—	1	2
Architecture	42	20	19	3	—	—	—
Building	29	13	14	2	—	—	—
Business Management	56	33	12	5	5	—	1
Catering	27	16	7	3	1	—	—
Chambers of Commerce	31	20	11	—	—	—	—
Chemical Engineering	17	17	—	—	—	—	—
Chemistry and Chemicals	28	20	7	1	—	—	—
Commerce and Trade...	16	13	2	1	—	—	—
Computers	20	10	4	5	1	—	—
Education	110	85	16	5	3	—	1
Electrical Industry ...	19	5	12	1	1	—	—
Electronics	36	20	14	—	2	—	—
Engineering	56	26	24	4	2	—	—
Estate and Estate Management ...	19	8	8	3	—	—	—
Exports...	27	14	10	2	—	—	1
Hospitals	35	27	8	—	—	—	—
Legal	38	31	6	—	1	—	—
Medical...	161	132	17	11	—	1	—
Metal Industries ...	21	5	16	—	—	—	—
Motor Trade	19	7	10	2	—	—	—
Municipal Works and Local Government ...	25	12	10	—	2	—	1
Printing...	18	7	10	—	—	1	—
Public Works and Construction and Civil Engineering ...	44	25	17	2	—	—	—
Science	140	122	17	—	1	—	—
Shipping and Marine ...	28	18	10	—	—	—	—
Sports Trade	15	10	5	—	—	—	—
Textiles and Drapery ...	31	21	9	1	—	—	—
Trade Unions	26	23	—	—	—	1	2
Transport	31	20	6	5	—	—	—
Travel	22	14	7	—	1	—	—
Wine and Spirit Trade	22	16	3	2	1	—	—
Total of the above ...	1,361	903	352	69	25	4	8
All others	860	577	237	36	5	1	4
Grand total	2,221	1,480	589	105	30	5	12

Source: Royal Commission on the Press 1974–77 from *British Rate and Data*, October 1974.

CHAPTER 2   THE FINANCES OF PERIODICALS

Consumers' expenditure

29. Table 19 shows that between 1965 and 1975, consumers' expenditure on magazines grew more slowly than that on newspapers. Consumers' expenditure on magazines measured in constant prices has fallen since 1965 so that expenditure on magazines has fallen from 0·21 % of gross domestic product (GDP) in 1965 to 0·18 % in 1975.

TABLE 19

CONSUMERS' EXPENDITURE ON MAGAZINES AND NEWSPAPERS, 1965–1975

Year	Magazines			Newspapers			Total consumers' expenditure
	Current prices £ million	Constant (1970) prices £ million	Implied price index (1970 =100)	Current prices £ million	Constant (1970) prices £ million	Implied price index (1970 =100)	Implied price index (1970=100)
1965 ...	67	98	68	195	300	65	80
1970 ...	102	102	100	266	266	100	100
1971 ...	104	93	112	318	268	119	108
1972 ...	123	99	124	354	270	131	115
1973 ...	126	100	126	369	276	134	125
1974 ...	141	93	152	442	261	169	145
1975 ...	164	79	208	557	249	224	179

Source: *National Income and Expenditure* 1965–75.

30. Table 20 shows IPC's estimates of consumers' expenditure on 'consumer' magazines by each major sector. No information is available for trade, technical

TABLE 20

CONSUMERS' EXPENDITURE ON 'CONSUMER' MAGAZINES BY SECTOR, 1965–1975

£ million current prices

Sector	1965	1970	1971	1972	1973	1974	1975
General Interest ...	35·9	52·0	60·2	70·3	78·1	92·8	114·4
Adult women's ...	20·7	26·3	27·3	31·6	33·0	39·0	46·7
Young women's ...	1·7	4·3	4·9	5·7	5·8	6·3	7·9
Teenage	2·9	2·9	3·0	4·2	10·0	6·2	5·9
Children's	12·0	15·5	16·8	18·1	17·8	17·1	19·9
Total	73·1	100·9	112·2	129·8	144·6	161·3	194·7

Source: IPC.

and professional journals. Table 20 shows the rapid growth in spending in current prices on young women's publications relative to the other sectors. The IPC figures for consumers' expenditure on 'consumer' magazines are greater than official statistics on consumers' expenditure on all magazines, and one reason for the difference is that their expenditure figures include overseas sales of 'consumer' magazines.

Advertisers' expenditure

31. Table 21 shows the trend of advertising expenditure in 'consumer' magazines and trade and technical journals over the period 1965 to 1975. Expenditure in trade, technical and professional journals has grown faster than in 'consumer' magazines. The share of all magazines and periodicals of total press advertising has fallen from 29% in 1965 to 24% in 1975. However, this is wholly the result of the fall in advertising in 'consumer' magazines from 16% to 12% of total press advertising.

TABLE 21

GROSS ADVERTISING EXPENDITURE ON ALL PERIODICALS, 1965–1975

Year	Magazines and periodicals(a)		Trade and technical journals(a)		All periodicals		All press	
	£ million	Index 1965= 100	£ million	Index 1965= 100	£million	Index 1965= 100	£ million	Index 1965= 100
1965	48	100	39	100	87	100	302	100
1970	51	106	53	136	104	120	400	132
1971	54	112	52	133	106	122	418	138
1972	60	125	61	156	121	139	498	165
1973	72	150	73	187	145	167	624	207
1974	71	148	80	205	141	162	649	215
1975	79	165	86	221	165	190	678	225

Source: Advertising Association.

Note:
(a) These are the Advertising Association's categories.

TABLE 22

INDICES OF MEDIA RATES, 1965–1975

	1965	1970	1971	1972	1973	1974	1975
Magazines and periodicals	82·5	100·0	108·9	110·4	113·3	132·0	160·2
Trade and technical journals ...	76·2	100·0	113·1	119·0	126·2	145·1	176·9
All press...	82·3	100·0	108·6	114·5	118·5	137·7	177·5

Source: Advertising Association.

TABLE 23

TOTAL REVENUE OF PERIODICALS FROM COPY SALES AND FROM ADVERTISING, 1972–1976

	1972		1973		1974		1975		1976(b)	
	£ million	%	£ million	%	£ million	%	£ million	%	£ million	%
'Consumer' magazines(a)										
Sales	88·5	62	98·3	61	108·5	63	129·7	64	141·1	62
Advertising	54·4	38	63·8	39	64·4	37	73·3	36	85·3	38
Total	142·9	100	162·1	100	172·9	100	203·0	100	226·4	100
Trade, technical and professional journals(a)										
Sales	31·4	38	33·6	36	39·7	38	47·2	40	60·8	41
Advertising	51·5	62	59·6	64	64·9	62	69·8	60	86·6	59
Total	82·9	100	93·2	100	104·6	100	117·0	100	147·4	100
All periodicals										
Sales	119·8	53	131·9	52	148·2	53	177·0	55	201·9	54
Advertising	106·0	47	123·4	48	129·3	47	143·1	45	171·9	46
Total	225·8	100	255·3	100	277·5	100	320·1	100	373·8	100

Source: *Business Monitor*, PQ485: Newspapers and periodicals.

Notes:

(a) The *Business Monitor* categories are 'trade, technical and professional' and 'other' periodicals.

(b) The 1976 figures are provisional.

32. The index of media rates shown in Table 22 suggests that trade, and technical journals have increased their rates by more than 'consumer' magazines but by the same amount as the press as a whole.

Sales and advertising revenues

33. Table 23 shows the split between sales and advertising revenues for 'consumer' and trade, technical and professional magazines over the period 1972 to 1975. The proportionate split was much the same in each of these years. But the split between circulation and advertisement revenue varies from year to year mainly as a reflection of changes in the advertising market. There has also been a long-term trend towards a greater dependence on circulation revenue. 'Consumer' magazines obtain approximately 35–40% of revenue from sales, and 60–65% from advertising. For trade, technical and professional publications the reverse holds: 60–65% of revenue is from sales and 35–40% from advertising.

34. Within 'consumer' magazine publishing itself, the sales/advertising split varies widely according to category and even within individual categories. Table 24 sets out approximate averages and ranges for the year 1973–74. The figures for 1976–77 would certainly be higher than those shown in Table 24.

TABLE 24

'CONSUMER' MAGAZINES: DEPENDENCE ON SALES REVENUE, 1973–1974

Proportion of total revenue derived from sales

Category	Average	Range
General	50	30–70
Women's weeklies	45	40–55
Women's monthlies	40	30–65
Young women's	40	30–80
Teenage	70	55–85
Children's	90	80–100

Source: Royal Commission on the Press 1974–77, based on trade estimates.

35. The relative dependence of 'consumer' and trade, technical and professional magazines on display and classified advertising is shown in Table 25. The figures suggest that there has been a substantial increase in classified relative to display advertising over the period 1960 to 1975.

Costs

36. No systematic enquiry has been undertaken by the Royal Commission into the cost structure of individual magazines, though they have received some information in confidence. Some publishers of academic and professional journals have specifically mentioned in evidence the burden of increased postal costs. Thus, the Royal Institute of British Architects (RIBA) state that between 1968 and 1974 the postage costs of the *RIBA Journal*, distributed mainly to subscribers, rose as a proportion of total production costs from 12% to 21%.

TABLE 25

REVENUE OF ALL PERIODICALS FROM DISPLAY AND FROM CLASSIFIED ADVERTISING(a), 1960–1975

	1960		1965		1970		1971		1972		1973		1974		1975	
	£m	%	£m	%	£m	%	£m	%	£m	%	£m	%	£m	%	£m	%
Magazines and Periodicals(b)																
Display	39	97	45	94	47	92	50	93	55	92	65	90	64	90	72	91
Classified	1	3	3	6	4	8	4	7	5	8	7	10	7	10	7	9
Total	40	100	48	100	51	100	54	100	60	100	72	100	71	100	79	100
Trade and technical journals																
Display	27	87	33	85	44	83	43	83	49	80	56	77	59	74	65	76
Classified	4	13	6	15	9	17	9	17	12	20	17	23	21	26	21	24
Total	31	100	39	100	53	100	52	100	61	100	73	100	80	100	86	100

Source: Advertising Association.

Notes:

(a) Financial advertising is minimal (less than £½m) in periodicals.

(b) These are the Advertising Association categories.

25

The British Medical Association in their evidence state that postage constitutes 27% of the cost of production and despatch of the *British Medical Journal*.

General profitability of periodical publishing

37. Table 26 shows the profitability of ten selected periodical publishing companies over the four years 1971–74. The picture is varied both between companies and over time.

TABLE 26

PROFITABILITY OF TEN SELECTED PERIODICAL PUBLISHERS, 1971–1974

Company	Sales 1974(a) (£ thousands)	Profit before tax(b) as a percentage of sales			
		1971	1972	1973	1974
Architectural Press (Holdings) ...	1,815	9·1	17·3	17·0	11·9
Benn Brothers	5,643	8·5	11·8	8·7	4·2
The Condé Nast Publications ...	3,594	3·2	8·2	11·4	7·0
Fuel and Metallurgical Journals Ltd.	1,109	5·9	7·3	3·2	—4·9
Ian Allen	983	10·0	9·0	7·7	1·2
IPC Business Press	37,684	7·0	6·7	5·8	4·6
IPC Magazines	70,978	5·9	6·2	6·1	5·1
Link House Publications	8,680	23·0	20·6	13·9	8·9
Morgan-Grampian	18,793	6·7	16·1	11·8	3·0
National Magazine Company ...	8,359	2·2	3·3	5·9	—3·3

Source: *Book and Periodical Publishers*, Business Ratio Report 1975 and 1976.

Notes:

(a) The years refer to financial years; thus 1974 refers to the financial year 1974/75.

(b) Net profits include interest and dividends receivable, but are before tax and other appropriations.

CHAPTER 3   OWNERSHIP OF PERIODICALS

38. The Royal Commission 1961–62 observed that:

> The range and diversity of the periodical press makes it difficult to measure the extent and significance of monopoly in this section of the industry. Spectacular movements towards concentration of ownership, culminating in the merger of the Odhams and Daily Mirror interests have certainly taken place since 1949. . . .[1]

39. The merger to which they referred led to the creation of the International Publishing Corporation (IPC)[2] which, in 1962, controlled an estimated 14% of 'consumer' magazine titles and about 7.5% of trade, technical and professional publications.[3] Since then, there have been no changes in ownership leading to a further significant increase in concentration and IPC's share of the market has

TABLE 27

THE 12 LARGEST PERIODICAL PUBLISHING COMPANIES ON THE BASIS OF NUMBER OF TITLES PUBLISHED, 1974

Company	Number of titles published		
	Total	'Consumer'	Trade, technical and professional
Academic Press	34	—	34
Argus Press Holdings	40	22	18
Benn Brothers	31	—	31
Blackwell Publications(a)	55	6	49
Cambridge University Press	49	2	47
IPC	213	120	93
The Mercury House Publications... ...	35	10	25
Morgan-Grampian	37	4	33
Oxford University Press	35	20	15
Pergamon Press	127	—	127
The Thomson Organisation	52	6	46
D C Thomson	32	32	—

Source: Royal Commission on the Press 1974–77 from *Newspaper Press Directory* and *British Rate and Data.*

Note:

(a) Blackwell Publications includes Basil Blackwell and Mott Limited and its associated company, Blackwell Scientific Publications Limited.

[1] Royal Commission on the Press 1961–62, *Report*, Cmnd 1811, 1962, paragraph 28.

[2] For details of ownership see Royal Commission on the Press 1974–77, *Final Report*, *Appendices*, Cmnd 6810–1, 1977, Appendix A.

[3] *Op cit*, footnote 14.

fallen in several categories, although it is still by far the largest periodical publisher. In this section, we examine the shares of the several periodical markets controlled by the larger publishers.

Number of titles controlled by the larger periodical publishers

40. The relative importance of the various periodical publishing companies can be assessed in a number of ways. The simplest but possibly least relevant indicator is the number of titles published by each company. As Table 27 shows, two companies stand out: IPC and Pergamon Press. IPC is strong in both 'consumer' and trade, technical and professional publishing, but Pergamon Press, as mainly a publisher of academic journals, only in the latter.

41. Although a head count of titles gives some indication of the main publishers, it is a poor way of measuring shares within each main periodical market. Shares of the market for 'consumer' magazines can be best expressed in terms either of consumers' expenditure on magazines or of total copies sold. In the trade, technical and professional press, the value of these measures is limited since many periodicals are distributed free: an alternative measure is the share of advertisng expenditure.

Market shares of 'consumer' magazines

42. IPC controlled the largest shares both of consumers' expenditure on and copy sales of 'consumer' magazines in 1975. It is estimated that, in 1975, the share of IPC[1] of consumers' expenditure was about 35% and of copy sales, about 37%. However, its share of each has fallen by about 10% since 1965. The second largest company in both 1965 and 1975 was D C Thomson with an estimated 20% of copy sales in both years; its share of consumers' expenditure is, however, much smaller. It is followed by BBC Publications and ITV Publications, each with about 10% of consumers' expenditure and of copy sales in 1975. Their shares are almost entirely due to the large circulations of the *Radio Times* and of the *TV Times*. The publications of the remaining 80 or so major 'consumer' magazine publishers amounted to little more than one-fifth of copy sales in 1975.[2] Among the larger publishers both for consumers' expenditure and sales are The Thomson Organisation, Associated Newspapers Group, EMAP National Publications, Reader's Digest Association, Paul Raymond Publications, National Magazine Company and Link House Publications.

43. Table 28 shows IPC's share of copy sales in each sector of 'consumer' magazine from 1965 to 1975. IPC's share of the market has fallen in all sectors except young women's titles, and particularly in adult women's titles.

44. In 1975, IPC controlled about 67% of the total copy sales of both adult and young women's magazines. Its nearest competitor was D C Thomson with about 20% of sales followed by The Thomson Organisation and the National Magazine Company which together accounted for only just over 6% of sales. IPC and D C Thomson own all the mass circulating adult women's weekly

---

[1] Including 'consumer' magazines published by IPC Business Press and Mirror Group Newspapers.

[2] The figures exclude about 60 small publishers which, in 1975, published less than two titles or had less than £100,000 of consumers' expenditure.

TABLE 28

THE PROPORTION OF THE TOTAL ANNUAL SALES OF 'CONSUMER'
MAGAZINES(a) CONTROLLED BY IPC(b), BY SECTOR, 1965–1975

Percentage shares of each sector

Sector	1965	1970	1971	1972	1973	1974	1975
General interest ...	24	21	20	19	18	18	16
Adult women's ...	87	76	74	73	72	70	68
Young women's ...	10	39	45	51	53	54	62
Teenage	59	47	44	42	58	50	47
Children's	42	40	41	45	41	41	40
All 'consumer' magazines	45	40	40	40	39	38	37

Source: IPC.

Notes:
(a) The shares relate to those 'consumer' magazines for which circulation data are available on a reasonably regular basis and estimates of circulation of children's titles.

(b) IPC's share includes 'consumer' magazines produced by IPC Business Press and Mirror Group Newspapers.

magazines. Although IPC has the largest share of sales of adult women's monthly magazines, The Thomson Organisation and the National Magazine Company have sizeable shares as well. The young women's, teenage and children's markets are also dominated by IPC and D C Thomson.

45. In the general and special interest sector, the two leading publishers are BBC Publications and ITV Publications each with about 20% of copy sales. IPC comes next with about 16% of copy sales, if *Reveille* (published by Mirror Group Newspapers) is included, and about 13% if not. Publishers with over 5% of copy sales include D C Thomson, Associated Newspapers Group and EMAP National Publications. It is in this sector, in particular, that the smaller publishers are also to be found.

Market shares of trade, technical and professional publications

46. For a number of reasons, it is difficult to examine concentration of ownership in the market for trade, technical and professional journals. Publishers tend to focus exclusively on certain, often narrow, areas of interest so that overall measures of concentration are less relevant. Moreover, the best indicator of concentration in the market for trade, technical and professional journals is the share of total display advertising expenditure, but this is useless for certain categories. like the academic journals, which carry little advertising. Thus, the importance of Pergamon Press, for example, is understated.

47. As Table 29 shows, if share of total display advertising expenditure is taken as the measure, IPC led the field in a number of categories of trade, technical and professional publications, notably agriculture, catering, electrical, radio and electrical goods, and transport. In 1975, IPC estimates that it obtained nearly 24% of net advertising revenue in the sector as a whole (see Table 30).

TABLE 29

THE PROPORTION OF TOTAL DISPLAY ADVERTISING EXPENDITURE IN ALL
TRADE, TECHNICAL AND PROFESSIONAL JOURNALS SPENT IN IPC JOURNALS,
BY 16 MAJOR CATEGORIES, YEARS ENDING MARCH 1972, 1973 AND 1974

Category	1972		1973		1974	
	Total Market	IPC's Share	Total Market	IPC's Share	Total Market	IPC's Share
	£m	%	£m	%	£m	%
Agriculture...	2·9	78·9	3·3	78·1	3·6	78·5
Aviation	—	—	2·1	13·0	2·2	14·7
Catering	0·7	66·8	0·8	65·8	0·8	63·4
Chemicals/Chemical Engineering	1·0	42·6	1·3	30·0	1·3	29·8
Construction	4·2	21·7	4·7	19·9	5·2	18·4
Electrical	0·6	78·0	0·7	71·4	0·7	70·7
Electronics and Control	1·4	24·5	1·5	27·0	1·7	34·1
Factory Equipment	3·4	34·2	3·6	32·0	3·5	28·0
Grocery	0·9	17·8	1·0	17·3	1·0	21·1
Marine	0·7	46·4	0·9	40·3	1·0	39·5
Motor Trade	0·7	25·0	0·8	24·4	0·9	22·1
Plastics	0·6	33·4	1·4	16·3	1·4	16·9
Radio and Electrical Goods ...	0·5	80·2	0·6	78·6	0·7	77·0
Transport	1·0	69·9	1·0	65·8	1·0	66·2
Travel	0·7	33·5	0·8	33·1	0·9	32·4
Women's Clothing and Home Furnishings	1·1	22·8	1·2	22·5	1·0	27·8

Source: IPC Business Press Ltd.

TABLE 30

NET ADVERTISEMENT REVENUE OF ALL TRADE, TECHNICAL AND
PROFESSIONAL JOURNALS[a], AND IPC's SHARE OF THIS TOTAL, 1965–1975

	1965	1970	1971	1972	1973	1974	1975
All publications £m	35·9	48·8	47·8	56·1	67·2	73·6	79·1
IPC's publications £m	11·9	12·4	12·6	13·2	15·5	16·6	18·7
IPC's market share %	33·1	25·4	26·4	23·5	23·1	22·6	23·6

Source: IPC Business Press Ltd.

Note:
   (a) Based on Advertising Association figure less 8% agent's commission.

CHAPTER 4   EASE OF ENTRY INTO PERIODICAL PUBLISHING

Births and deaths of periodicals

48. Table 31 shows that, using the *Newspaper Press Directory* (NPD) as the source, there were 4,256 recorded changes in periodical titles over the nine years 1966 to 1974; a figure which is roughly the same as the total number of titles listed in NPD in 1974. There were 1,013 births and 892 deaths of 'consumer' magazines, and 1,317 births and 1,034 deaths of trade and technical magazines. The annual number of births and deaths is also shown in Table 31.

TABLE 31

BIRTHS AND DEATHS OF PERIODICALS, 1966–1974

Year	'Consumer' magazines			Trade, technical and professional publications		
	Born	Died	Net change	Born	Died	Net change
1966...	93	71	+ 22	72	72	0
1967...	90	121	− 31	138	103	+ 35
1968...	59	79	− 20	125	96	+ 29
1969...	111	92	+ 19	131	107	+ 24
1970...	173	124	+ 49	180	118	+ 62
1971...	102	105	− 3	155	139	+ 16
1972...	142	74	+ 68	200	116	+ 84
1973...	123	89	+ 34	176	131	+ 45
1974...	120	137	− 17	140	152	− 12
Total ...	1,013	892	+121	1,317	1,034	+283

Source: Periodical Publishers Association's evidence to the Royal Commission on the Press 1974–77 using an analysis compiled by IPC Marketing Services from *British Rate and Data*.

49. According to an IPC research monograph, "the very high figure of births and deaths of magazines tends to be inflated because of the many small publications that have a fleeting life; they bravely appear, only to disappear after a short time. They will therefore be recorded as both a birth and a death".[1] But, in some areas publishers tend to launch magazines with a short life expectancy, and to replace ailing titles by new ones if sales begin to flag. This obviously increases the number of births and deaths. The 1961–62 Royal Commission on the Press noted that periodicals were "much more ephemeral than newspapers. They cater for constantly changing fashions and habits, and they come and go with frequency which if it were found in the newspaper press, would indicate an alarming instability".[2]

[1] IPC, "The Mass Media—The Audience", *Sociological Monographs*, number 9.
[2] *Op. cit.*, Cmnd 1811, 1962, paragraph 13.

Changes in 'consumer' magazine titles

50. Within the sectors of 'consumer' magazine publishing there is considerable variation in the number of births and deaths. Table 32 shows that, even among those 'consumer' magazines which have published circulation figures,

TABLE 32

BIRTHS AND DEATHS OF 'CONSUMER' MAGAZINES[a] BY SECTOR, 1965–1975

Sector	Number of titles		Number of births 1965–1975	Number of deaths 1965–1975
	1965	1975		
Adult women's				
Women's weeklies	9	11	4	2
General	6	8	3	1
Feminine interest	13	13	7	7
Home interest	7	9	6	4
Total	35	41	20	14
Young women's				
General	1	5	4	—
Romantic fiction	10	14	5	1
Total	11	19	9	1
Teenage				
General	7	6	3	4
Pop	—	3	7	4
Total	7	9	10	8
Children's				
Nursery comics	7	9	18	16
Humorous comics	8	13	13	8
Boys' adventure	12	15	21	18
Soccer comics	—	1	6	5
Girls' adventure	4	7	9	6
Educational comics	5	2	3	6
Junior TV guides	—	1	1	—
Total	36	48	71	59
General interest				
Politics and current affairs ...	7	14	8	1
Popular general interest	6	7	1	—
Home entertainment guides ...	9	4	—	5
Religion and mysticism	17	15	1	3
Sex	3	10	8	1
Classified advertising	3	3	—	—
Pop	4	7	4	1
Gardening	5	6	2	1
General motoring	12	12	3	3
Soccer	2	2	4	4
Other	125	157	44	12
Total	193	237	75	31
Grand total	282	354	185	113

Source: IPC.

Note:

(a) Includes all titles for which circulation data are available on a reasonably regular basis and children's titles for which circulation data are not available.

there have been 181 births and 109 deaths over the period 1966 to 1975, equal to 46% of the sum of titles in 1965 and 1975. A high level of title turnover can mean (a) that the market is expanding or contracting; or (b) that it is unstable so that demand is continually changing requiring corresponding adjustments by publishers in terms of title names and market strategy; or (c) that there has been a large number of unsuccessful attempts at entry into an otherwise stable market.

51. The highest proportions of title turnover are in the teenage and children's sectors. In some categories, such as young women's titles, there have been few closures but many launches since 1965; in others such as home entertainment guides, there have been more closures than launches. But many categories within the general interest sector show remarkable stability.

Ease of entry

52. Table 33 shows the number of adult women's, young women's and general interest titles launched since 1966 which had circulations of over 300,000 in 1974. A total of 33 titles were launched by 20 publishing houses. Of these, IPC alone launched nine titles, followed by Haymarket Publications with four. None of the other companies launched more than two titles.

TABLE 33

NUMBER OF 'CONSUMER' MAGAZINES WITH CIRCULATIONS OF OVER 30,000 IN 1974 LAUNCHED BETWEEN 1966 AND 1974, AND THE PUBLISHERS WHICH LAUNCHED THEM

Publisher	Total	General interest	Adult women's	Young women's	Sex magazines
British European Associated Publishers	1	—	1	—	—
Fontessa Publications	1	—	—	—	1
Galaxy Publications	1	—	—	—	1
Haymarket Publications	4	4	—	—	—
IPC	9	4	1	4	—
Link House Publishing Co.	1	1	—	—	—
Mercury House Publications	1	1	—	—	—
Model and Allied Publications	2	2	—	—	—
MS Publishing	1	—	1	—	—
National Magazine Company	2	—	2	—	—
Parkers Price Guide Limited	1	1	—	—	—
Pinehurst Limited	1	1	—	—	—
Paul Raymond Publications	1	—	—	—	1
Retail Journals	1	—	1	—	—
RF County Magazines	1	1	—	—	—
Slimming Magazine Limited	1	1	—	—	—
Spotlight Publications	1	1	—	—	—
The Thomson Organisation	1	—	1	—	—
Time Out Limited	1	1	—	—	—
Top Sellers	1	—	—	—	1
Total	33	18	7	4	4

Source: Royal Commission on the Press 1974–77 from *Newspaper Press Directory* and *British Rate and Data.*

53. This evidence suggests that smaller publishers can successfully launch a new 'consumer' periodical if they are able to identify a gap in the market, but there can be little doubt that the larger companies are better placed to incur the

considerable costs that are required to enter some markets. The greatest opportunities for launching a new title are likely to exist either where the market is expanding or where new interests are developing among readers. It is also often important to launch a title at the right moment in the advertising cycle. Needless to say, the large companies like the small have their failures; notable examples are the two women's weeklies launched by IPC since 1965, *Candida* and *Favourite Story Weekly*.

Launch costs

54. Detailed information about the cost of launching a new publication is not publicly available, but clearly the risks vary tremendously. It would be extremely expensive to launch a new mass market magazine; it might now cost £1 million to launch a new women's weekly, and £500,000 a new women's monthly.

55. A major distinction is whether the new magazine is to be 'long-term' or 'opportunist'. The former are magazines which have been launched with the objective of establishing a long-lasting and valuable asset. In general, such magazines are costly to launch, and it usually takes over a year to recover the initial costs. Most of the costs are for promotional expenditure both before the launch and during the early months in which circulation is being built up. 'Opportunist' publications on the other hand, are launched to take advantage of a sudden boom in a particular market and are short-term ventures. Such a magazine must be launched very quickly with little preparation and its publisher must be ready to close it before it enters a loss. Launch costs are lower and, if the magazine is successful, they are recovered quickly.

56. The sectors in which it is easiest to launch a new title are probably those of teenage and children's publications. Many publishers in these fields have adopted a policy of rapid change, and titles are launched with only a short life expectancy, to be merged with others as the latest fad fades. When a title's circulation begins to fall it is generally better to launch a new title with new appeal, and to merge the old title into it, than to try to re-establish the circulation of the existing title by promotional expenditure. Conversely, if the new title is a complete failure, then it can be merged with an existing one, which may even increase its sales enabling most, if not all, of the launch costs to be recouped. This cost-saving policy of 'launch and merge' is, of course, open only to those publishers who are already established in the market.

57. Ownership of printing facilities probably has little or no effect on ease of entry because contract printing facilities are readily available and are commonly used by periodical publishers.

Conclusions

58. The initial launch costs of a long-term publication are often high, and it will generally be necessary to bear a loss for over a year before it breaks even. This suggests that entry to some markets is limited. With 'opportunist' publications the risk of failure is also high, but with good timing and lower and more quickly recovered launch costs, the rewards can also be substantial. This market is more open to the smaller companies. The other study in this volume—that on the alternative press—shows that in non-commercial publishing it is possible successfully to launch new publications often appealing to very limited audiences with only a small amount of initial capital. It is, however, much more difficult to make the transition from this kind of publishing to the more commercial world.

Part II
The Alternative Press

Table of Contents

Appendices

List of Tables

The role of the alternative press is to produce news and information using criteria of selection which are relevant to its readers. However objective an editor is there is inevitably an element of selection into important and unimportant, and unless that editor has an understanding of what motivates his readers he will inevitably get his priorities wrong in the view of those who are more interested in alternatives to existing society than in the established society. So a demand for an alternative press is established.

Anthony Wigens, Editor, *Counter Culture*, Letter to the Royal Commission on the Press, 1976.

CHAPTER 1 INTRODUCTION

1. The growth of publications not normally regarded as belonging to the 'established' press has in recent years attracted considerable attention. To observers who have viewed this growth largely as an offshoot of the 'underground' culture of the sixties, the appearance of such publications has been insignificant, of moment only to participants in that culture. But to others, a large and diverse output of small publications is an indication of some inadequacy on the part of established papers and periodicals. There is nothing new in an alternative press, although there are no means of telling how large it was in earlier periods. The few alternative papers which still survive from pre-war days provide evidence of a persistent tradition of small radical publications. Stanley Harrison identifies some hundred or more factory-floor papers produced by militants on the shopfloor at the height of the General Strike of 1926.[1] The vast majority were short-lived, and ceased publication almost as soon as the Strike was over. Many in the alternative press world of today are aware of their links with the radical journals in the early years of the nineteenth century of William Cobbett, T J Wooller, Henry Hetherington, and with many other authors of the 'unstamped' papers which fought the battle for the abolition of the stamp duty during the 1830s. But the alternative press in the nineteenth century was by no means restricted in its contents to radical or labour politics. Among mid- and late-Victorian publications were many like G J Holyoake's feminist and secular *Reasoner*, or *Beeton's Christmas Annual* which became ardently republican after 1872, or *The Adult: A Journal for the Advancement of freedom in Sexual Relationships* which appeared in 1897.

2. The existence of an alternative press is important for two reasons. First, the right of minorities to publish their views without undue difficulty is at the heart of the freedom of the press. Second, one of the functions of a press in a democratic society is to reflect and impart the opinions of the widest range of articulate interests.

3. A multiplicity of alternative publications suggests dissatisfaction with an insufficiently diverse established press, and an unwillingness or inability on the part of major publications to provide space for the opinions of small minorities. On this view, the alternative press provides at least some of the diversity lacking among stable and respectable publications. One purpose of the present study is to test this assertion by reference to:

   (*a*) the number of alternative publications;
   (*b*) their purposes;
   (*c*) their readership; and
   (*d*) their economic condition and, in particular, the ease with which they can establish themselves in the market.

4. If it can be shown that the total number of readers or the range of interests of the alternative press is very small, then it may be argued convincingly that the established press could meet minority needs with little additional space or effort. On the other hand, if there are many readers and interests, it would not be reason-

---

[1] *Poor Men's Guardians: A record of the struggles for a free democratic newspaper press 1763–1973*, Lawrence and Wishart, London, 1974, page 198.

able to expect the established press to cater for all their concerns, and there would be good grounds for ensuring that minority publications can survive. We therefore analyse the economics of these publications and the obstacles which they must overcome before achieving a sure footing in the market.

Problems of definition

5. When the Royal Commission first considered the alternative press, the suggestion was made that it would be enough to study some half dozen well-known publications which claim to present alternative points of view. But this could not have indicated the range of titles or subjects covered, and it was decided to undertake a more extensive sample survey. Choosing the papers to be included in the list from which the sample was to be drawn presented a major problem. There is no accepted definition of an alternative publication. Indeed, a number of those actually included in the sample took the view that they should not be included under this head. One possible definition would restrict the field to the 'undergound' publications, most of which had their origins in the nineteen-sixties and are most often associated with the life-style surrounding the popular music of that decade, with its emphasis on personal freedom, especially with regard to sexual relationships and the use of drugs. A more comprehensive definition would include any publication seeking to meet a need not catered for by commercially-published newspapers and magazines.

6. The first definition mentioned above is narrow, as well as presenting border-line problems. During the late sixties and early seventies there were many 'underground' publications, but only a few remain. Such a definition would leave out many magazines, such as *The Ecologist* and *The Spokesman*, which would certainly not count as 'underground' but which are proud of their adherence to alternative viewpoints and regard themselves as part of the alternative press.

7. On the other hand, if the net is cast wide, different difficulties emerge. At what point, for instance, do long-running, soundly based publications cease to be alternative? For instance, one of the sampling frames used in the survey included *Freedom*, an anarchist weekly founded in 1886. If the field is held to include any publication which espouses views or deals with subjects not given regular coverage by publications generally available at newsagents, not only would the magazines already mentioned be brought in, but also the large number of community newspapers which have been started in recent years as well as specialised journals of all sorts, many of which are 'alternative' to more widely read publications.

8. We decided to include community papers because their origins and attitudes are often similar to those of the more obviously 'alternative' press. Frequently, they are founded because some local people feel that local issues and viewpoints are not being adequately aired in existing papers, or because they reject the approach taken by the local established press. By the measure of numbers and influence it can be argued that community papers in fact constitute the most important part of the alternative press, and we therefore carried out a special investigation of them.

41

9. In deciding what other alternative publications to include, we found that criteria based on circulation, longevity or method of production would not have allowed us to compile a reasonably comprehensive list of publications. When we compiled the list from which the sample was drawn, titles were generally included because they had appeared on the lists of others working in the field. Where judgments had to be made about whether to include a title, we took into account important factors such as the expression of attitudes hostile to widely-held beliefs, and a basically non-commercial approach to publication. We stress that we did not adopt a strict definition, and that the list is therefore neither consistent nor fully representative.

Size of the field

10. The ephemeral nature of many alternative publications makes accurate estimates of the total numbers impossible. Mr John Noyce has recently completed a *Directory of British Alternative Periodicals* for the period 1965–74, in which he lists over 1,250. [1] He himself agrees, however, that this is by no means complete. For instance, his list does not include the bulk of the left-wing political periodicals. Of course, many of the papers listed are now defunct, but the total shows clearly that a very large number of alternative publications still exists; the *Directory* suggests about 500, and a list culled from various other published guides (see paragraph 12) confirms this order of magnitude.

---

[1] John L. Noyce, *Directory of British Alternative Periodicals 1965–1974*, 1976.

CHAPTER 2 THE SURVEY

11. Although some research into the alternative press has been carried out in the course of producing directories, there is as yet no systematic basis for assessing its quality, aims, or condition. We carried out a postal survey early in 1976 which aimed at filling this gap. The questionnaire[1] was backed up by interviews with editors and others.

The sample

12. Mr Noyce's new directory was not completed until after our sample had been drawn from a list of 500 publications taken from the following sources:

   (a) *Alternative England and Wales* (Nicholas Saunders), London 1975.

   (b) Community Levy for Alternative Projects (CLAP), *Handbooks* 2–9.

   (c) John Noyce's earlier and much shorter *Directory of Alternative Periodicals*, Smoothie Publications, 1974.

Originally, the sample contained 40 publications. However, it proved so difficult to achieve a reasonable rate of return that a second sample of the same size was drawn in order to increase the amount of available information. The papers in the two samples are listed in Appendix B.

13. To supplement the basic information derived from the questionnaire, the newer Noyce *Directory* was used as the base for a further 10% sample which yielded 126 titles. This provided details of the number of titles launched in each of the last ten years, their length of life, and their frequency of publication. These details were taken from the *Directory*, and the publications were not approached. Where appropriate, the results of this inquiry have been incorporated in those from the main survey.

Response to the questionnaire

14. Questionnaires were completed by 26 of the sample of 80, a rate of return of 34%. Of the other 54, 12 were subsequently identified as having gone out of business. In ten instances the Post Office marked the letter "Not Known", and in one case "Demolished". One publication decided not to co-operate. We obtained details of three other publications included in the sample from other information which they gave to the Royal Commission. The majority of the remaining 27 presumably received the questionnaire but took no further action. The failure or disappearance of at least 23 of the sample of 80 periodicals is a vivid demonstration both of the volatility of this type of publication, and of the speed with which a list of them is likely to become out of date. The low rate of return means that our findings must be treated with due caution. Nevertheless, we consider that the survey gives a reasonably representative picture of the alternative press.

15. The 26 respondents were:

Political and nationalist

   Anti-Apartheid News
   Liberation
   Pacifist

---

[1] Reproduced as Appendix A.

The Spokesman
Red Weekly
Spanish Workers Defence Committee Bulletin
Cornish Nation
Planet
Free Palestine
Free Ireland

Community papers

Bright Times (Brighton)
Lowdown (Brentwood)
Angell (South London)
Leigh People's Paper
Gateshead Street Press
The Bugle (Liverpool)

Philosophy

The Atlantean
Towards the Infinite
The Grimoire of the Holy Partners

Science and technology

The Ecologist
Undercurrents

Others

Counter Culture (life-styles)
Gladrag (homosexual)
IT (general/news)
The Other Half Lives (women's lib)
Up against the law (civil rights)

The quality of the returns varied considerably. Five gave only the minimum possible information but six papers provided a great deal more information than we requested. In several cases, the questionnaires were returned only after the editorial committee had discussed whether or not they wished to become involved in any way with the Royal Commission. Although one publication decided not to participate, most of those who replied explained that they thought it unreasonable to complain about "the establishment's" lack of interest and then to refuse a request for information.

16. The three other publications in the sample about which we obtained information were:

Gay News (homosexual)
Time Out (London guide)
West Highland Free Press (community)[1]

In addition, a questionnaire was completed by the Leicestershire Rural Community Council whose papers were not included in the sample, giving details of

---

[1] The *West Highland Free Press* is much more like a conventional local weekly newspaper than many other community newspapers and is indeed classified as a weekly newspaper in *Concentration of Ownership in the Provincial Press*, Cmnd 6810–5, 1977.

some Leicestershire community papers as examples to answer the questions. These have been incorporated in the results as if they were one paper.[1] The total number of publications for which survey results are given is therefore 30.

Scope of this study

17. In the following chapters, we record our survey findings. We begin by estimating the lifespan and the range of alternative publications on the basis of the survey results; then we describe in more detail some of the publications themselves. We go on to examine the economics of the alternative press, in particular, its distribution. Finally we suggest some of the conclusions which may be drawn from this survey.

---

[1] Leicestershire's community newspapers are described in Chapter 4.

CHAPTER 3 LIFESPAN AND RANGE OF TITLES

Lifespan

18. We have already seen that there are probably about 500 alternative publications. Table 1 shows the number and date of launches of papers in the 10% sample taken from John Noyce's *Directory*[1] (the 'Noyce sample') and from the replies to our survey.

TABLE 1

ALTERNATIVE PRESS LAUNCHES, 1965–1975

Year	Noyce sample		Royal Commission survey replies	
	Number	%	Number	%
Pre 1965	3	2	3	10
1965	0	0	1	3
1966	1	1	0	0
1967	0	0	0	0
1968	1	1	3	10
1969	9	7	0	0
1970	16	13	6	20
1971	22	18	1	3
1972	23	18	6	20
1973	9	7	4	13
1974	9	7	2	7
1975	5	4	1	3
Exact date not known				
At all	13	10	3	10
1960s	2	2	0	0
1970s	13	10	0	0
Total	126	100	30	100

Note: Percentages are given, despite the low numbers involved, in order to allow the results from the two different sources to be compared.

19. Table 1 suggests that launches of alternative publications reached a peak in the early 1970s and have since declined. At the time of our survey 47 out of the 126 in the Noyce sample were known to be continuing publication. Taking only the 95 publications of which the starting date was known, we found that eight lasted only one year, three two years, two three years and two four years. One had lasted for six years and 32 of the 95 were still in print. The life of 32 publications could not be ascertained from the *Directory*. Two publications known to have been started at some time in the 1960s were still continuing in 1976 as were six from the 1970s, and seven for which no indication of the launch date was given.

20. The questionnaire survey showed that 22 out of the 30 publications were still alive in 1976. This rather high figure should be qualified by a reminder that, in the great majority of cases, questionnaires were returned for publications which were still in existence, because we found it very difficult to contact those who had been concerned with papers which had folded. Of the six publications which had collapsed, two had lasted for one year, three had folded in the same year in which they were started, and the lifespan of one could not be discovered.

[1] *Op. cit.*

21. The Noyce sample provides the better indication of the lifespan of alternative publications. Although some were very short-lived, many which were started in the last ten years have survived and seem to have established a stable readership. This suggests that they are meeting a genuine demand. Moreover, it seems that most alternative publications appear or have appeared at regular intervals. Table 2 suggests that monthly publication is the most common by a considerable margin, followed by quarterly, although, on the basis of these samples, over one-fifth appear only irregularly. Nearly all the community papers in our survey appeared monthly.

TABLE 2

FREQUENCY OF PUBLICATION

	Noyce sample	Royal Commission survey replies
	%	%
Weekly ...	16	8
Fortnightly ...	11	12
Monthly ...	29	34
Quarterly ...	22	15
Six monthly ...	—	4
Yearly ...	—	4
Irregularly ...	22	23

Note: Percentages based on those publications for which the information is known.

Range of titles

22. The major categories of alternative publication can be seen from Table 3 which breaks down our samples into nine categories. The size of the sample in each category was based on the estimated total number in each.

TABLE 3

BREAKDOWN OF ROYAL COMMISSION SAMPLES INTO NINE CATEGORIES

Subject	Number of papers in samples
Politics	24
Community papers	19
General topics	12
Philosophy	7
Science and technology	6
Gay	4
Nationalist (UK and foreign)	4
Women's lib	3
Unidentifiable	1
Total	80

CHAPTER 4 COMMUNITY NEWSPAPERS

Survey findings

23. Community newspapers are probably the largest category of alternative publication. Those included in the survey[1] were all either weeklies or monthlies. The majority were produced using off-set or photo-litho, although it was common for a paper of this sort to have started life as a duplicated sheet. They were produced almost entirely by volunteers and none exceeded 15p in price. The actual size of paper varied, although on average they had 10–12 pages on either A4 or 16 in. by 12 in. paper. The number of copies sold varied between 100 and 8,500. However, four of the eight papers in question sold in the region of 2,000 per issue. Distribution was by hand, by street selling, or through local news-agents. Although the appearance of most of these community papers was far from amateurish, the standard of layout and presentation was, if anything, lower than that of other categories. This may in part reflect the more limited scope and resources available to community papers. Replies to the survey suggest that the function of the community press is to provide information about local events; to foster a sense of community, particularly for newcomers to a district; and to provide a platform for debate about local issues and for the expression of local views which might otherwise be lost in less localised discussions. These objectives can be of interest to all sections of a community and, because they might not otherwise be fulfilled, the community press performs an important function. It is also the one section of the alternative press which still seems to be gaining momentum, at least as evidenced by the enthusiasm apparent in the returned questionnaires, whereas in the field as a whole the number of launches seems to be declining.

TABLE 4

DATES OF KNOWN LAUNCHES OF COMMUNITY PAPERS 1969–1975

	Noyce sample *Number of titles*	*Royal Commission survey* *Number of titles*
1969	1	0
1970	2	1
1971	7	1
1972	8	1
1973	1	3
1974	1	2
1975	1	0
Total	21	8

24. The eight community papers which replied to the questionnaire all saw themselves as offering a genuine alternative to the established papers in their areas. All were dissatisfied with the way in which the other papers treated local

[1] See paragraph 16.

49

affairs. In particular, the established press was criticised for not carrying out its 'watchdog' functions effectively when it came to such matters as investigating allegations of corruption among local committees. A few respondents suggested that the established press was too closely tied to interest groups, and some regretted the lack of a left-wing national daily. In general, though, the community papers were very much more concerned with building up what their promoters regard as fair and adequate treatment of local issues than with the political colour of the national press.

25. The community papers did not seem to have run into some of the difficulties faced by other alternative papers. The replies mentioned occasional legal snags, usually over the reporting of court cases, and one of the more successful papers said that the 'established' local paper had first applied pressure to discourage them from publishing and had then tried to buy them out. Advertising appears, from the sample, to be hard to come by, being limited to local concerns and to free placements for suitable local events. Advertising revenue tends to be very low. The survey suggests that the main problems, particularly in the early stages, are a lack of volunteers to do the often time-consuming work, and a lack of experience and knowledge. On the other hand, distribution, which causes difficulties for most of the alternative press, does not worry community newspapers because they circulate in small areas.

26. The Royal Commission identified the category of community papers within the alternative press as making a particularly useful contribution to the diversity of voices within the press as a whole. We therefore decided to undertake a special study. Our further inquiries consisted of visits to Leicestershire and Islington, and correspondence with the Department of the Environment and the Association of Metropolitan Authorities about the nature and extent of local authority assistance to community newspapers.

Community newspapers in Leicestershire

27. Leicestershire now has 22 community newspapers in rural areas. Many of them were started in order to campaign on a specific local issue and have since grown to meet other needs of their communities, though others stemmed from a more general sense of community need. Most are run by a Board, usually composed of all the staff and an independent chairman, with specific appointments to the jobs of editor and of advertising, accounts and distribution managers. Copy is submitted by the staff and by occasional contributors. None of the staff is paid and the papers are produced in spare time. Most of the papers appear monthly, ranging in size from eight to thirty pages. Duplicators are used to produce the smaller circulation papers (in some cases with electronically cut stencils), but those with circulations of upwards of 3,000 are generally printed by off-set litho. The duplicated papers are usually paid for but the printed ones are often freesheets with all their revenue coming from advertising, which takes up about one-third of the paper. In these cases, advertising revenue needs to cover printing costs plus 10% for other expenses. Total production costs for an eight-page A4 paper would be about £220 per issue of 3,000 copies at 1977 prices. Methods of distribution vary. In small communities, local newsagents often deliver free of charge, or in return for free advertising. In more scattered areas, distribution is usually done by hand by the staff. We were told that there were great advantages in making the paper free and thus achieving a

very high penetration among households. Only in this way could the paper be sure that it was reaching a fair cross-section of the community and it would also be able to attract higher advertising revenue. Local District and Parish Councillors were said to accept that the papers were doing a useful job despite their frequent criticism of Council decisions, and the papers have also made it easier to pass information to the community. Apparently, relations with the County Council have not been so good. We were told that officials at this level often appeared to ignore the community newspapers, or to regard them as a nuisance, and some feared lest the papers came to perform too many of what were properly the Parish Council's tasks.

The Leicestershire Community Newspaper Advisor

28. The present Leicestershire Community Newspaper Advisor is based on the Rural Community Council, which is financed by the Development Commission, and has a remit to foster rural community life. One of the threats to the rural community has been seen as arising from the increase of commuting into Leicester from outlying villages. The *Leicester Mercury*, the local evening newspaper, has been criticised as being remote from the needs of readers in small communities. Accordingly, community newspapers are helped in their task of counteracting what some regard as adverse trends.

29. The present Advisor is paid by the Rural Community Council, partly from the excess revenue of the *Blaby Courier*, for which he has worked part-time. (The *Blaby Courier* was one of the first community papers in the area.) He told us that the main difficulty in setting up a community newspaper was lack of experience and that very often a group wanted to set up a local paper but did not know how. The Advisor has helped by explaining what the most suitable organisational structure might be, by detailing the major costs, and by outlining the arguments for and against a cover price. He could also suggest the best way to set about getting advertising, and explain the basic technical points about layout and printing. Although there has been no shortage of jobbing printers in the Leicester area, apparently very few of them have wanted to take on work for an inexperienced, potentially unreliable group of people. But we were told that if a printer was assured that the community newspaper had access to advice he was usually much more willing to take on the work at a reasonable price. The Advisor has also set up two-day training sessions for people involved in producing community papers. These have covered both the production and editorial sides, and have been found very helpful.

30. In dealing with running a paper, the Advisor's main task has been to encourage the promoters to broaden their appeal and not to cater for particular interest groups. This has often meant encouraging a group to take on more people and to cover wider interests. In turn, of course, width of appeal helps to attract advertising. Once the paper has established itself, the role of the Advisor diminishes, although his availability has been helpful if papers come up against such problems as how to deal with a potential clash with the local council or to avoid legal difficulties. The Advisor's office then becomes a source of 'common services' for all the papers.

Community newspapers in Islington

31. In Islington (Greater London), the local authority itself provides support and advice to a large number of community newspapers. The majority are

tenants' news sheets, usually based on a limited area like a particular estate, and run by a small and committed group of residents. In sharp contrast to Leicestershire, most of the papers are politically far to the left. They range from three-page duplicated news sheets to professional printed newspapers. The best known, and most successful, of the community papers in the Borough is the independent *The Islington Gutter Press*. It usually runs to about 24 pages and costs 3p and does not generally carry advertising.

32. The Council provides assistance through its own Information Department and, more usually, through its Participation Section. This was set up to promote tenant participation in a wide range of activities, one of the more important of which has turned out to be community papers. The Section has made available duplicating facilities where this method of production is most suitable, although there is apparently no difficulty about finding printers to undertake the work. The most important function has been the provision of advice on how to start a newspaper and on technical matters.

33. The most important difference between the Islington and Leicestershire papers is that the Islington papers do not carry advertising. We were told that their promoters felt that the inclusion of advertising would place unacceptable and inevitable constraints upon what the paper could write, and that it was better not to take advertising at all than to try to be selective about it. Because the costs of starting such papers are very low, it has been possible for the Council to provide support without any difficulty. There have been a few cases of Councillors complaining about the content of certain papers. However, the Participation Section told us that not only was no undue pressure brought to bear by the Council on editorial content (although they had on occasion "explained things") but also that in an urban area with a highly fragmented population, only the local authority could administer such support.

Local authority powers to assist the community press

34. Although one attempt to clarify the law in early 1976 was abortive, it seems clear that local authorities are able to give financial assistance to community newspapers under their existing general powers of discretionary expenditure.[1] Islington Borough Council considered that they had ample powers for assistance and pointed out that this could be given as part of their various social services expenditures.

Discussion

35. Our inquiries revealed wide differences both in the types of newspapers in Leicestershire and in Islington and in views about how they should operate. To some extent, they reflect no more than rural and urban differences. But there are also sharp political differences which affect the promoters of the newspapers. Nevertheless, there was general agreement over the need for community newspapers, the value of what they achieve, and the broad nature of their aims. Our interviews with those concerned in both areas also confirmed such important points as the very low costs of starting papers, and the absence of any major

---

[1] For example, section 137 of the Local Government Act 1972 allows local authorities the discretion to spend up to the product of a rate of 2p in the £ on anything "which in their opinion is in the interests of their area or any part of it, or all or some of its inhabitants".

difficulties over printing and distribution. The main difficulty which stands out from this further investigation is the lack of experience and technical knowlege among groups who wish to start their own paper. This has been common to Islington and Leicestershire, and points to the need for some form of advice on how to start and run a community paper, which seems to be the most useful form of aid that can be offered. There remains the question of the form which advice should take and where it should be available. In a short survey conducted for the Royal Commission by the Association of Metropolitan Authorities, 11 authorities said that they already gave assistance of one sort or another. Eight of these were in London. In all, 43 authorities replied. Thirty-two said that they did not give such assistance and, of these, 28 said that they had never been asked, and three said that they could not afford to help even if asked. The 11 which gave help to community papers usually provided printing facilities, duplication equipment, or small cash grants. Three of the authorities (Greenwich, Hammersmith and Islington) specifically mentioned help given by their social workers. Thus, some local authorities are already aware of the usefulness and importance of community newspapers and willing to make help available when it is requested. The cost of this is very low and most of the help which papers need fits in with work already being undertaken by most local authorities. Officials in Islington argued that in urban areas there was no other body capable of providing assistance of this sort. They also expressed the belief that it was possible for community newspapers to remain more 'independent' and free to criticise when funded by the local authority than when dependent upon advertisers and subject to commercial pressures.

36. Against this must be set the views of Leicestershire's Community Newspaper Advisor, who believed that it would be impossible for the papers in his area to criticise so freely if they were dependent upon the County Council or even on District Councils for support. He also suggested that the position of an Advisor paid by the local authority would quickly become untenable, and it was clearly implied by 'participation' workers in Islington that they, too, had difficulties in this respect. The quantity and quality of editorial content in the Leicestershire papers does not suggest the insuperable difficulties in taking paid advertising that were feared by the Islington officials, although it may be that in urban areas there is not the same scope for local paid advertising by small shops and the like as in a country district. Where advertising is available, it can be argued that there is no need for any other form of aid, since the Leicestershire experience suggests that costs can be recovered from this source, provided that the people who produce community papers are unpaid.

37. The Royal Commission deals with the question of aid to community newspapers in Chapter 13 of its Final Report.[1]

---

[1] Royal Commission on the Press 1974–77, *Final Report*, Cmnd 6810, 1977.

CHAPTER 5   OTHER ALTERNATIVE PUBLICATIONS

Political and nationalist papers

38. Political and nationalist papers formed the largest group in our samples. They were a diverse set of publications ranging from *The Spokesman*, a six-monthly journal of some 120 pages costing £1.50, to an occasional bulletin issued free by an organisation based in Paris. Most of the papers in this category of our sample had between 12 and 16 pages. Preference over page size was evenly divided between A5 and 16 in. × 12 in. For all but one, the cover price was 10p or 15p. Most were sold by post, with street sales as the second most common method. Sales figures were often only estimated but, of our respondents, four papers sold in the region of 1,100 per issue, and four others each sold 6,000, 7,000, 9,000 and an estimated 15,000 per issue. All of our sample were affiliated to a larger organisation; none was an independent journal of opinion, although in one case the affiliation was primarily ideological rather than institutional. This indicates that minority political groups think it very important to have a publication devoted specifically to their cause. Those which returned questionnaires were all on the left and scattered across the spectrum from full-blooded Marxism to mild socialism. Some of them were founded just to campaign on a particular issue but others moved from one campaign to another; a few had wider interests and aims and these had also lasted the longest. Our survey suggests that part of the function of the alternative press is to speak on short-term issues; but this is not new and goes back to the factory floor papers of the General Strike and beyond.

39. These papers were critical of the established press. One editor went so far as to assert that "the established press represented the views of perhaps four people". When asked for their comments on what the Royal Commission should seek to reform, two editors suggested that steps should be taken to ensure that a wider range of viewpoints was reflected in the established press, and one considered that the entire newspaper industry should be nationalised and put under workers' control. He also put forward the view that access to the presses should be guaranteed for everyone, in proportion to the amount of support for their views.

40. As far as their commercial policies were concerned, none carried more than a bare minimum of advertising, although all but one said that they had no ideological objection to it. All were prepared to accept financial support provided that no strings were attached. Two editors were particularly concerned that the system of postal charges should be changed. In most cases, relief from commercial anxiety stemmed from the security of being an integral part of a parent political organisation.

41. Despite the growth of political nationalism in the United Kingdom both *Planet* (Welsh nationalist) and *Cornish Nation* concentrated very much more heavily on the cultural than on the political life of their respective areas. Both were published in English but supported the case for their 'national' languages. Both were exceptionally professional in appearance. *Cornish Nation* had 32 pages, sold for 20p, and was printed on A4 paper. *Planet* had 52 pages, again A4, and cost 40p. It received about £800 per annum from the Welsh Arts Council which, the editor conceded, made possible its present high quality.

Both papers were dissatisfied with the treatment which their chief interests received in the established press. The editor of *Planet* was particularly disturbed by regional and local press monopolies and by the difficulties which faced small publications. He also expressed a preference for subsidies for such elements of newspaper production as paper and postal charges rather than for direct subsidies to individual publications.

42. *Free Ireland* and *Free Palestine* had run into several legal difficulties. Both papers declared that their purposes were entirely reasonable and non-subversive. *Free Palestine* claimed a wide network of contacts in the Arab World. Both editors complained of the hypocrisy of the established press and one thought it "parochial". *Free Ireland* had no funds and was now defunct, having only printed one edition. *Free Palestine* had been running for eight years, had a considerable degree of international support and considered that it "would never be allowed to go under".

Papers devoted to philosophy

43. The samples contained three publications in this category. *The Atlantean* was a magazine of comparatively long standing, having been founded in 1957. It was published quarterly with 20 small size pages, cost 30p and had a circulation of about 600 copies. *Towards the Infinite*, launched in 1971, was a relative newcomer. It appeared bi-monthly at a cost of 16p, with about 36 small size pages per issue and sales of 250. The third, *The Grimoire of the Holy Partners*, was largely a one man venture; its frequency of publication and price fluctuated according to demand. All these magazines depended on postal distribution for their sales. *The Atlantean* and *Towards the Infinite* were prepared to take advertising, but preferred matter related to their interests. In fact, they contained very little in the way of advertising, commercial or otherwise. Neither of them had views on what was wrong with the established press or how it should be reformed. They gave the impression of magazines catering for small, fairly stable readerships, working within tight but adequate budgets, and little concerned with issues outside their own interests.

Papers concerned with alternative science and technology

44. The two papers in this category are both comparatively well known, with circulations in the region of 10,000. At the time of our survey, *Undercurrents* contained 48 pages for 45p, and *The Ecologist* had 36 pages and cost 40p. The former was at first published quarterly but changed to bi-monthly, whilst the latter was issued ten times a year. In appearance they were (apart from *Time Out*) the most sophisticated in the sample. Both were printed on A4 paper and had 'glossy' covers.

45. In defining its objects, *The Ecologist* said that its overriding theme was that "some problems—poverty, over-population and pollution, crime and violence —cannot be solved by technological methods because they treat symptoms rather than causes, and thereby create more problems than they solve, and also because they are logistically inapplicable on anything but an insignificantly small scale". *Undercurrents* said that the aim of the magazine was "to promote Radical Technology, a synthesis of Alternative Technology—technology based on renewable resources—and anarchist socialism".

46. Both were prepared to accept such advertising as could be reconciled with their objectives. The one major difficulty had been a lack of cash, which had delayed one issue of *Undercurrents*. Both publications depended very largely on postal distribution and postal charges constituted about 35–40% of their costs. Both were concerned at the costs of postage.

47. Although neither publication put forward any detailed suggestions for reform, the editor of *Undercurrents* criticised the "straight press" because "it confuses its self-interest—to survive in the comfort to which it is accustomed—with the public interest—freedom of the press. The subsidies required to keep the heavyweights afloat could be used to launch quite literally thousands of new titles".

Papers dealing with other topics

48. The 'General topics' category in our survey included a women's liberation paper, two gay papers, an educational venture aimed at bringing alternative values to the notice of schools, a publication concerned with individuals' legal rights, and the long running, if irregular, *IT*, and *Time Out*. We discuss *Time Out* and *Gay News* in the following chapter. Although the gay category emerges from the sample as relatively small, other evidence suggests that it is in fact one of the fastest growing areas, since a large number of the local groups of the Campaign for Homosexual Equality print their own papers.

49. All except one paper in this group were priced in the 10–15p range. The exception was *Up against the Law* which had a variable price depending upon whether the buyer was a private individual (30p) or wanted it in connection with his business, profession, or on behalf of an organisation (90p). In size they ranged from 4–36 pages but all used either A4 or A5 paper except for *IT* which was printed on 18 in.×12 in. Sales varied between 75 and 9,000 per issue. Two were above 5,000, two below 200, and one between 400 and 500. The most usual method of distribution was through alternative bookshops, with a certain amount of additional selling by hand at such events as pop festivals. There was very little postal distribution. All the papers in this section reported difficulties over distribution, which two of the publications regarded as the greatest single obstacle to success. In one case, the distributors were criticised for failing to notify the paper of actual sales soon enough for print runs to be adjusted. Two publications had tried and failed to get W H Smith to handle them. The 'general topics' publications carried most news, and several of them used the various 'alternative' newsagencies. The People's News Service was the most used, although the Release organisation and other alternative papers were also sifted quite regularly for news.

50. This group seemed to be more commercially aware than some of the other papers in our survey. However, *Counter Culture*, the publication intended as an educational venture, would not accept advertising, since it was "part of the existing culture". This was also a purely private, one-man venture, printed on presses belonging to his own small business. It was interesting that once the planned series of topics had been covered, the editor decided to turn to the community paper field, and had just produced a trial free news sheet which had predominantly environmentalist aims.

51. Three of the publications in this group were affiliated to parent organisations. One had ceased publication because of lack of finance, but had been replaced by a duplicated free news letter. The papers concerned with sexual behaviour were highly critical of the treatment of sexual topics in the established press. They strongly condemned sensationalism and innuendo, often unfounded, about an individual's sexual relationships.

52. The history of *IT* illustrates an unusual degree of persistence to keep a particular publication going. *IT* was originally founded in 1966 but folded in 1972, re-emerging as *Maya* in 1974 and then as *IT* again ("incorporating *Maya*") in 1975. The editor had clear ideas as to the direction in which he hoped the paper would move, and was aiming at its becoming a Sunday weekly. He was critical of the "narrow range of opinion" in the established press at present, and had experienced legal difficulties which once led to his spending four weeks in prison for contempt, after publishing a banned advertisement.

Time Out

53. Although *Time Out* started life in 1968 as a broadsheet akin to many alternative papers of the late sixties, it has since built itself up to a circulation of some 50,000, largely in Greater London. It is therefore much larger than any of the other publications which we have examined. It provides an example of an alternative publication finding a gap in the market, succeeding, and becoming part of the established press. In this respect it is very unusual and justifies detailed discussion.

54. At the time when the magazine first appeared, there was no real awareness of a major market gap to be filled. The owner, Tony Elliott, and his friends started the magazine with only £70 capital. The first three issues were of 5,000 copies each and distributed by them. The fourth issue was accepted by the distributors, Moore-Harness, who have handled the magazine ever since. To start with, *Time Out* appeared once every three weeks and was produced by four people. It became a fortnightly after a year, and then, in 1971, went over to weekly publication and changed to its present format. By this stage, there were about a dozen staff and some 25,000 copies were printed for each issue. *Time Out* now employs about 50 people, of whom about one-third work only part-time for the magazine. About half of *Time Out*'s production costs are now met from advertising revenue, and it is trading profitably with an annual turnover of over £500,000. W H Smith sell the magazine subject to a weekly affidavit that it contains nothing which might lead to legal action against them.

55. *Time Out* divides into three parts. About half its 84 or so pages are given over to advertising, and about 30 pages are made up of lists of events. The listings are free to anyone who wishes to send in the necessary information. The remainder of a typical issue is made up of editorial pages. Editorial policy aims to cover as wide a range of topics as possible, with a preference for subjects which are of interest to Londoners, and which are in some way unusual. Politically, the magazine is generally regarded as having a left-wing slant, although it is not tied to any particular party or group and is not seen by its editor as professing a particular political view point. The most popular parts of the magazine are the film and music listings. The features, reviews, and news items are also widely read.

56. Recent readership surveys undertaken for *Time Out* reveal that the magazine now reaches some 8% of all adults in Greater London (13·3% of the 15–34 age group) and that it now sells best to people normally regarded as 'up market'. Eighty per cent of its readers are under 30; 68% live in Central London; and 40% earn between £1,800 and £3,500 per annum after tax. Sixty-four per cent of *Time Out* readers read *The Sunday Times*, 42% *The Guardian* and 32% *The Times*.

57. Mr Elliott does not regard *Time Out* as an alternative magazine any more. In his view, his has become a young, small publishing house whose roots are those of an alternative publication launched in the 1960s, an origin still reflected in some of the magazine's articles. It has published two London guides, and attempted a full-scale commercial launch of a new magazine *Sell Out*, which failed partly because of lack of pre-launch market research and partly because of a failure to appreciate the size of the sums needed to keep it afloat in its early

stages. Nevertheless, when it closed, *Sell Out* had a circulation of about 18,000 per issue. *Time Out* itself has in the past had serious financial problems. From 1970 to 1972, it suffered cash-flow difficulties and accumulated debts of about £30,000. At that point, Mr Elliott considered that *Time Out* was almost certainly insolvent and survived only as a result of the goodwill and co-operation of its printers and other creditors. These debts were paid off over the next year. Mr Elliott has suggested that the sum of *Time Out*'s debts was roughly equivalent to the amount of capital needed to launch a viable publication.

58. Mr Elliott told us that two changes would be particularly helpful to small publishers. Public money or financial guarantees could be made available to the press, and used to some extent to support young houses through the most difficult early period. In his view, it would also be very helpful if the laws relating to publications, including libel, were to be changed, so that the publishers alone were held responsible for the content of their publications. The present system whereby publisher, printer and distributor were equally liable made the problems of young and, in particular, the more unusual publications in finding printers and distributors unnecessarily great.[1]

59. The origins of *Time Out* are similar to those of many alternative publications and its experience suggests that:

(a) there is no such thing as a single definable break-through point for small magazines;

(b) distribution is of fundamental importance;

(c) for a publication not backed by a major publishing house, or sympathetic treatment from banks regarding overdrafts, financial backing to tide over early difficulties is essential, but difficult to find, luck playing a major part;

(d) experience has to be gained the hard way—and it may again be a matter of luck that mistakes are not followed by collapse.

Gay News and *Private Eye*

60. Two other magazines which began life as alternative publications and which have achieved considerable success are *Gay News* and *Private Eye*. The first issue of *Gay News* was produced in mid-1972 and the magazine has appeared fortnightly ever since. In their evidence to the Royal Commission,[2] the publishers explained that the magazine was founded by a group of people who had no experience whatsoever of running any sort of business, let alone a newspaper. They said that if they had had any experience, *Gay News* would probably never have been started. The magazine is now trading profitably and has a circulation in the region of 18,000–20,000 copies per issue with an estimated readership four times that size. *Private Eye* was originally founded in 1962 and also appears fortnightly. It is probably the best known publication dealing with political and social events to be launched from outside the conventional publishing world. At one time, its circulation was over 100,000, larger than the United Kingdom circulation of any of the established journals of opinion.

---

[1] See further paragraph 76.

[2] Part of *Gay News*' evidence which deals with distribution difficulties is reproduced as Appendix C.

CHAPTER 7 ECONOMIC ASPECTS OF THE ALTERNATIVE PRESS

61. In many cases, respondents were not able to provide a detailed economic breakdown of the costs and income of their publication. However, 15 returns contained enough financial information to give a reasonable idea of their publication's position. It is also important to note that seven publications acknowledged financial help from a parent or associated organisation, and this made it difficult to estimate the true state of the publication's own finances.

Starting capital

62. Eight publications said that they had capital to start with. Four began with between £30 and £60, one with £450, and the remaining three had sums of £200, £2,500 and £5,000. Each of the latter three publications belonged to a larger organisation. All eight were still in business in 1975.

Cover prices

63. Prices varied from 3p, a community weekly, to £1.50, a political six-monthly. The majority were in the 10–40p range. As might be expected, price depended largely on the frequency of publication and the sort of topic covered, with the specialist or semi-technical publications tending to charge more than the community papers and proselytizing journals.

Circulation

64. Table 5 shows the results of the questionnaire concerning circulation.

TABLE 5

RANGE OF CIRCULATION OF ALTERNATIVE PAPERS

Circulation range (thousands)	Number in range	% of those answering
0–0·5	6	24
0·5–1	3	12
1–2	8	32
2–3	0	0
3–4	0	0
4–5	1	4
5–6	1	4
6–7	2	8
7–8	1	4
8–9	1	4
9–10	0	0
More than 10	2(a)	8
Total	25	100

Note:
(a) 11,000 and an estimated 15,000.

Income

65. Estimates of the income of different publications derived from the questionnaire were difficult because in most cases respondents were uncertain or imprecise about the amount received from counter sales as opposed to

subscriptions. Where advertising revenue was involved, the figures were more precise. Nine publications acknowledged income from other sources, such as parent or affiliated organisations and donations, but only in respect of *Planet*, which received £800 from the Welsh Arts Council, was it possible to discover exactly how much was involved. Only two had received support from the Community Levy for Alternative Projects (CLAP), showing how hard it is for this voluntary scheme to make an impact.[1] These amounts were not specified.

66. Table 6 (which excludes *Time Out*) shows income per annum for those publications which supplied this information and demonstrates the small part played by advertising in the alternative press. Of the nine publications receiving less than £5,000 from advertising, seven received less than £150, and only one received more than £1,000.

TABLE 6

NUMBER OF ALTERNATIVE PAPERS WITH SPECIFIED INCOMES PER ANNUM FROM COUNTER SALES, SUBSCRIPTIONS AND ADVERTISING(*a*)

Amount	Counter Sales	Subscriptions	Advertising
Less than £5,000	11	10	9
£5,000–£10,000	1	2	1
£10,000–£15,000	2	0	0
More than £15,000	2	1	0

Note:
(*a*) Many publishers had only a hazy idea of the state of their finances. The data in this table were calculated from a figure per issue and grossed up to give an annual figure.

Costs

67. The questionnaire asked for details of printing, paper and production costs, together with details of pay for production staff where appropriate. As has already been noted, only a very few of the alternative publications in the sample paid their staff, and of the two which did, one spent £800 and the other £7,000 per annum. In assessing staff costs, it is important to bear in mind that in several cases the people who produce the publication are in fact employed and paid by the parent organisation. Table 7 shows printing, paper and production costs per issue related to size of circulation.

Advertising

68. Alternative magazines carry little advertising and this is significant when explaining their financial difficulties. Obviously there are publications which, given their aims, could never hope to attract much advertising and therefore make no attempt. However, the figures given for advertising space and revenue show that, as yet, neither advertisers nor the alternative press attempt to make much use of each other.

---

[1] The Community Levy for Alternative Projects (CLAP) is a scheme to encourage businesses, other organisations and individuals to donate financial support to alternative projects. Projects needing support can advertise in the CLAP *Handbook*, and those wishing to help send money direct to the project. CLAP was started in 1975. Its *Handbooks* have been published bi-monthly as supplements to *Peace News*.

69. Nineteen out of the 27 returned questionnaires showed that the publication in question carried advertising. Table 8 shows the percentage of space given to advertising in the 12 papers which answered the relevant question.

TABLE 7

PRINTING, PAPER AND PRODUCTION COSTS PER ISSUE RELATED TO CIRCULATION

Circulation range (thousands)				Number of titles in this range	Average printing, paper and production cost per issue of these titles (£)
0–0·5	...	...	...	4	33
0·5–1	...	...	...	3	158
1–2	...	...	...	6	481
2–3	...	...	...	0	—
3–4	...	...	...	0	—
4–5	...	...	...	1	500
5–6	...	...	...	1	480
6–7	...	...	...	2	625
7–8	...	...	...	1	1,400
8–9	...	...	...	1	500
9–10	...	...	...	0	—
More than 10 ...		...	...	1	2,200
Total ...		...	...	20	—

70. Advertising rates ranged between £200 a page for a paper with a circulation of 9,000 to 50p a page for a paper with a circulation of 1,000. Some papers provided free space for suitable advertisements. One group (600–1,800 circulation) charged about £10 per page, another (1,300–7,500 circulation) charged in the region of £45 per page, and one (5,500 circulation) charged around £100 per page. Where column inches were used as a measurement of rate, the figure was in every case between 75p and £2.00. Classified advertisements were usually free; where a charge was made, it varied between 2p and 5p a word. There does not appear to be any general scale based on circulation, although the need to set rates according to what the market will bear is recognised. Although it might be difficult for the alternative press to attract highly paid advertising, there certainly appears to be scope for publications to try to attract more and to be better organised for handling it.

TABLE 8

PROPORTION OF SPACE GIVEN OVER TO ADVERTISING

% of paper					Number of papers
0–10	...	...	...	...	8
10–20	...	...	...	...	2
20–30	...	...	...	...	2

Distribution

71. Previous chapters have shown that the various types of publication use a number of different methods of distribution. However, it is the experience of most groups that distribution is the most difficult problem that has to be overcome. Several of those in the survey used a 'distributor'; the main one being Moore-Harness Limited. Distributors supply copies to wholesalers or, in some cases, themselves act as wholesalers. Although other distributors have been used by the alternative press in the past, only one other, a small firm called AMD Ltd, was used by any of the papers in the survey. After the survey had been completed, we visited the Distribution Co-operative which was set up in 1976 as a co-operative enterprise to make it easier for left-wing newspapers and magazines to achieve cheaper and more satisfactory distribution. This organisation did not exist when the questionnaires were returned. The distributor, Paperchain Limited, is also now used by a number of alternative publications.

72. Some publications depend very heavily on postal distribution, and almost all of those complained about postal charges. Because most distribution organisations are reluctant to handle publications with small circulations, it is likely that they will be the worst affected by high postal charges. The categories in the survey for which postal charges posed the greatest problems were the scientific and technological papers and those dealing with philosophy, although there were instances in every category. Almost no alternative papers could register as newspapers, so that they would receive a first-class service for second-class rates.[1] The other most frequently used methods were street and hand selling, and local shops, not necessarily newsagents. The latter were particularly important to the community papers, which occasionally found it difficult to find enough willing hands. This did not, however, emerge as a major problem.

73. Those publications which used a national distribution service paid the distributor 55% of the cover price. The only other form of distribution where any discount was involved was retailing through local shops and newsagents. Ten publications specified the rates agreed with distributors or retailers, ranging from 20% to 66%. No explanation was apparent for this surprisingly wide spread, though it may reflect the varying levels of willingness on the part of retail outlets to put up with the trouble of handling small publications. There were several community papers, for instance, which were apparently handled free by local shopkeepers.

74. The costs of distribution can be high, and the survey showed clearly that magazines which wish to achieve a nationwide distribution often find considerable difficulty in doing so.[2] In their evidence to the Royal Commission, W H Smith said that circulations of between 5,000 and 10,000 copies per issue are needed before they will take a publication. But they added that: "It would not be true to say that the WHS share of minority papers is well below the company's share of the market as a whole. In fact, it is probably above, because

---

[1] The requirements for registration as a newspaper with the Post Office include weekly or more frequent publication and a content not less than one-third or which consists "of political or other news or of articles relating thereto or to other current topics". Postal distribution is discussed in the Royal Commission's *Final Report*, Cmnd 6810, 1977, paragraphs 8.29–8.32 and 13.45–13.46.

[2] See, for example, the evidence of *Gay News* included as Appendix C.

in many cases WHS takes bulk supplies to cater for other wholesalers' small orders." Moore-Harness, too, are known to apply a commercial criterion which is similar to that of W H Smith.

75. Mr Ken Coates, the editor of *The Spokesman*, summarised the problem very clearly in a letter to the *Times Literary Supplement*,[1] describing the experience of *The Spokesman* when it tried to publish two books, one a special edition of Khruschev's secret speech to the 20th Congress of the Soviet Communist Party, the other Medvedev's *History of Stalinism*. It was expected that "a few thousand of each title might sell"; W H Smith, however, refused to handle them. Mr Coates' comments might have been made about the fate of serious alternative magazines and newspapers.

> We think we do appreciate the decision of W H Smith in this matter. We were asking them to distribute a few hundred copies of titles, the interest in which would be rather specialised. Clearly a large concern would find such an operation far more unprofitable than the mass distribution of popular works of fiction. Nevertheless, both Smith's and us are now caught in a serious dilemma. Because in large parts of the country no other serious outlets for paperback books exist, people living in the areas served exclusively by Smith's shops will be unable to obtain our books in the normal manner. Perhaps there is a point at which a minority is so small that it can have no legitimate claim upon the established amenities of publishing and distribution. But the Medvedev works are of extraordinary importance to every serious student of Soviet affairs. That they should be partially suppressed, however inadvertently, as a result of a quasi-monopoly in books distribution, can hardly be the wish of anyone in the publishing trade. The level of profit which results from the distribution of small or intermediate orders must, in present circumstances, clearly influence distributors when deciding whether to act: yet the constant concentration and centralisation of effective powers in publishing is bound to pose recurrent problems of this kind for freedom of speech. In this case it would be absurd to accuse W H Smith of deliberate censorship. Nonetheless, caught as they are in a particular economic logic, the outcome remains one which is grossly harmful to freedom of expression. It is ironic that these books, prohibited in the USSR for political reasons, may only achieve a limited circulation in this country as a result of commercial pressures.

76. However, in addition to economic considerations, distributors are faced with the problem of their legal responsibility for the content of publications and their possible liability in the event, for example, of an action for defamation. It has been suggested[2] that, if legal responsibility rested exclusively with the editor and/or publisher, the willingness of distributors to handle alternative publications would be greatly increased. The question of distributors' liability is dealt with in the final Report of the Royal Commission,[3] which recommends a relaxation in the conditions of the special defence of innocent dissemination currently available to distributors.

---

[1] *Times Literary Supplement*, 4th June, 1975.
[2] See, for example, paragraph 58.
[3] *Op. cit.*, Cmnd 6810, 1977, paragraphs 19.39–19.46.

CHAPTER 8 SUMMARY AND CONCLUSIONS

77. The results both of the sample drawn from John Noyce's *Directory*[1] and of the Royal Commission's Survey show that the alternative press is active and flourishing in many fields. Indeed, what emerges most clearly is the sheer diversity of topics covered as well as of types of publication.

78. The details of launches and lifespans suggest, however, that the increase in the number of new publications is not now as high as it was in the early 1970s. 1971 and 1973 appear to have been peak years and, while it is difficult to evaluate the social factors behind this, it may be significant that these were years of economic boom. The subsequent decline may have been in part the result of the downturn in the economy rather than of fully satisfied demand. It may also have resulted in part from a realisation by the established press that some needs were not being met, and that such values as ecological concern and sexual permissiveness which were largely the preserve of the alternative press in the late 1960s and early 1970s had become more widely accepted.

79. The community papers emerge as the group with the most energy and the fastest growth rate at present. It is significant that this enthusiasm seems to have been sustained, for the moment at least, and that several community papers which returned questionnaires mentioned new ventures in their localities. This suggests that there may be a renewed increase in the number of launches. The popularity of community papers is relatively easy to explain in terms of need, since their objectives command fairly widespread support. They achieve them in two different ways. One is to concentrate on printing information which is too localised in many cases for inclusion in even a small circulation local weekly, and certainly in a regional paper. The other is to take as their subject matter more obviously 'alternative' ideas and ways of life. In some ways, they appear to be at a disadvantage, since their promoters often lack experience and knowledge and find it hard to raise money, particularly in deprived areas. A few of them have received help from the Community Levy for Alternative Projects (CLAP), but such help is very limited and CLAP seems unlikely ever to be able to provide support on a large scale.

80. Of the other categories in the survey, the most sophisticated and well organised are the two alternative science journals, closely followed by certain of the publications in the general category. Whereas the scientific and philosophical magazines depend mainly on postal distribution, the community papers use local shops and hand selling. The papers concerned mostly with general topics and news are most likely to use 'alternative' bookshops and hand selling at selected sites. In circulation terms, the biggest are the semi-scientific and the general topics categories, the smallest the community papers. That, of course, is more or less decided by their respective functions. Only the group of political and nationalist papers seemed to be financially secure. This is largely because they are so often linked to larger organisations which are prepared to provide financial support in return for having a printed outlet for their views. Even so, a number of them pointed out that they too suffered, in some cases badly, from difficulties of distribution, which beset all the publications other than the community papers. The distribution problems are, in brief, the difficulty of finding retail outlets and a nationwide distributor and, the level of postal charges.

---

[1] *Op cit.*

81. The survey gave a reasonably clear picture of a typical organisational framework adopted by the alternative press. Eleven of the 27 said that they were run by an editor, another 11 by some form of editorial group, described either as a committee or as a collective. Four publications had an editor who was advised by a small committee. The predominantly amateur nature of these publications was illustrated by the fact that only six said that they employed professional journalists in either a part- or full-time capacity. One of these six employed two journalists, another four.

82. The survey also cast light on some of the other problems of the alternative press and on the perceived shortcomings of the established press. Changes which were proposed as of direct benefit to the alternative press included changes in the laws of libel to exempt distributors, printers and retailers, who could otherwise use the risk of a lawsuit as an excuse to refuse to handle a publication; a better distribution system for small magazines; changes in the system for registering newspapers with the Post Office; and the placing of government advertising in alternative publications. There was also almost complete agreement that financial help would only be welcome provided that there were no strings attached. It was not made clear whether 'strings' applied only to editorial policy and content, or to the general management of the paper as well. Three publications expressed doubts about accepting money from local or central government; two of these suggested that trust money would be preferable. Although very few publications reported any brushes with the law, the interviews with editors suggested that they were well aware of the pitfalls which lie in that area. The *OZ* trials, one of the most celebrated instances of an alternative publication running foul of the law courts, have obviously not been forgotten.[1]

83. As might be expected, there was unanimity over the failure of the established press to deal adequately with the interests of the respondent publications. The level of interest in possible reforms and even in willingness to comment varied considerably. Many publications either preferred to make no comment or wished to remain quietly in their existing niches. Of those who commented some thought that the established press did what it set out to do reasonably well, but that its ambit was not sufficiently wide, hence the need for alternatives. Others were more critical and said that the established press was biased against various groups, superficial, sensational, parochial and an organ of capitalism. Understandably, comments tended to be related to the particular interest of the publication replying. When asked what reform was needed, some were general, suggesting that the established press should be free of all forms of pressure and that it should be open to everyone to contribute his views, or that it should be run democratically, as a workers' co-operative.

---

[1] See further, Tony Palmer, *The Trials of OZ*, Blond and Briggs, London, 1971.

Appendices

THE ALTERNATIVE PRESS
QUESTIONNAIRE

Name of publication:

Address:

————————

1.   How often does the newspaper/magazine appear?

2.   When was the first issue?

3.   Has it appeared regularly ever since then?

4.   Has the newspaper/magazine ever appeared under any other title?

5.   How many pages on average does the newspaper/magazine contain?

6.   What size page do you normally use?

7.   Could you give a short, general idea of the newspaper/magazine's aims? How far do you consider those aims are being fulfilled? What particular difficulties have you encountered in achieving your objects? Has the paper gone through any 'crises of survival'?

8.   Is the newspaper/magazine affiliated to a political party or group? Or to any other body (eg a Community Association)?

9.   Do you have connexions with any other publication?

10.   Who owns the premises on which the newspaper/magazine is produced?

11.   How many people are regularly involved in producing and distributing the paper?
    (Sub-divide: a. Editorial and Production
                   b. Contributors
                   c. Distributors)

12.   Can you give any estimate of the average number of hours a week they work, individually and in total? (Sub-divide as 11, if possible.)

13.   Does the paper have an editor? Editorial collective, etc?

14.   Do any of the main people involved in producing the paper have a full-time job in journalism, advertising or the media?

15.   What method do you use to produce the paper? (Duplicator, photo-lithography, etc).

16.   Do you use outside contractors to print the paper? Or for any other part of the production process?

17.   Have you ever experienced problems in finding a printer?

18.   How many copies of the paper's latest issue did you have printed?

19.   What distribution and retailing methods do you use? (Post, street-sellers, newsagents, etc.) Could you estimate the proportion distributed and sold by each method?

20.   Have you encountered any difficulty in having your publication distributed?

21. (Where relevant.) Do your distributors receive their supplies on a discounted cover-price basis? If so, which discounts apply, and what is the retailer's share? If not, could you describe your system?

22. Could you estimate the number of copies of the last issue that remained unsold?

23. How much does the newspaper/magazine cost to buy?

24. Is there a special subscription price? If so, how many subscribers do you have?

25. What is the average net income from sales revenue per issue? What was the income from sales of the latest issue?

26. Do you accept advertising? (If not, why not?)

27. What proportion of space, on average, is occupied by advertising?

28. Could you give details of advertising rates?

29. What is the average net income from advertising per issue? What was the income from advertising in the latest issue?

30. Do you have any other (regular) sources of income apart from sales and advertising revenue? (Eg council support.)

31. Would you accept financial support from the local council, or Government, or any other source, if it were offered?

32. Have you ever received any money through CLAP (Community Levy for Alternative Projects)? If so, when and how much?

33. Are any of the people involved in the production of the paper (except for outside contractors) paid? If so, could you say how much?

34. Do any of the people involved in the production of the paper regularly contribute money to keep the paper going?

35. How much capital did you have to start production? What equipment, etc did you buy?

36. Can you give details of average expenditure per issue on paper, printing, and other costs?

37. Have you ever used the People's News Service, or any of the other alternative news services, as a source of information for your paper?

38. Are there any plans to change your paper in the near future in any way? If so, what are they? Do you want to become a regular, above-ground publication on the *Time Out* basis?

39. Do you have any particular legal problems?

40. What criticisms do you have of the established press?

41. What aspects of the press do you consider the Royal Commission should most seek to reform?

First sample
1. The Atlantean
2. Azania Combat
3. Birmingham Street Press
4. Black and Red Outlook
5. The Black Worker and his World
6. Brecht Times
7. Cambridge Scene
8. Confrontation
9. Cumbria Free Press
10. The Ecologist
11. Free Palestine
12. Gateshead Street Press
13. Gay News
14. Gladrag
15. The Grimoire of the Holy Partners
16. Impulse
17. Inside Story
18. IT
19. Keep Left
20. Leigh People's Paper
21. Liberation
22. Living as Women
23. Manningham News and Views
24. Oppositionist
25. Ore
26. The Pacifist
27. Paper Tiger
28. Rebel
29. Red Camden
30. Red Weekly
31. Seeds
32. Solidarity
33. The Starry Plough
34. Tenants' News
35. Towards the Infinite
36. Tuebrook Bugle (Liverpool)
37. Undercurrents
38. Up Against the Law
39. Women's Liberation Review
40. Workers' Press

Second sample

1. Angell
2. Anti-Apartheid News
3. Big Flame
4. Bright Times
5. Chapeltown Community Newspaper
6. Claimants
7. Come Together
8. Communus
9. Cornish Nation
10. Counter Culture
11. Doris
12. Elysian
13. Free Ireland
14. Glasgow News
15. International Socialism
16. Kite
17. Latin American Review of Books
18. Lowdown
19. Lunch
20. New Left Review
21. Nirvana
22. North Gloucestershire Free Press
23. Ostrich
24. Planet
25. Real Time
26. Red Rat
27. Red Vanguard
28. Revelation
29. Romano Drum
30. Roundabout
31. Socialist Worker
32. Spanish Workers Defence Committee Bulletin
33. Straight
34. The Other Half Lives
35. The Spokesman
36. Tillydrone News and Views
37. Time Out
38. West Highland Free Press
39. Workers News
40. Write First Time

APPENDIX C

EXTRACTS FROM THE EVIDENCE SUBMITTED TO THE ROYAL COMMISSION BY *GAY NEWS*

Distribution

There is not much point in putting time, effort and money into producing a publication if you cannot get the publication into the hands of potential readers. It is in the field of distribution that we have the greatest doubts about the present situation.

When *Gay News* was founded, it was sold by members of the staff in gay pubs and at gay social gatherings. A considerable number of our copies are still sold through these channels. We have about 3,000 postal subscriptions and the balance are sold through newsagents.

Until *Gay News* had been publishing for almost 18 months, it was impossible for us to find a distributor who was prepared to accept the handling of *Gay News*. At that stage Moore-Harness Limited took on the distribution and have continued to distribute us ever since. They have looked after us very well and are continuing to do so. However, they would undoubtedly agree that it is extremely difficult to get nation-wide distribution for a small publication, and perhaps some large ones too, and unfortunately, we cannot think of alternative distribution arrangements. However, our impression is that the distribution of publications is controlled by far too few companies. We have very little impression of much competition. It is, therefore, our experience that if, as is so in at least one part of the country, a wholesaler has, for instance, very strong views against homosexuality it is virtually impossible for a gay publication, however well produced and however legal, to be distributed in that area. We consider this highly undesirable.

Inevitably, any discussion about the distribution of publications leads to the immense power of W H Smith. It may be of interest to you to know the attitude of a small publication such as *Gay News* to W H Smith. W H Smith have been accused of taking a very moralistic attitude towards publications. This may have been so in the past. However, it has been our experience that their reluctance to handle *Gay News* until a few months ago was based purely on commercial considerations. It was our impression that they thought there was no great market for *Gay News*.

At present W H Smith are selling *Gay News* in a few selected outlets. We, from our extremely biased viewpoint, consider that they are being far too slow and cautious and that they should be selling *Gay News* in every branch. We fully understand their position, however, and should specifically confirm that we, in our dealings with them, have found no misuse of their virtually monopoly position in this field. However, having said that, we should certainly welcome any suggestions your Commission might make to encourage greater competition and efficiency in the whole field of periodical distribution.

Printed in England for Her Majesty's Stationery Office by Harrison & Sons (London) Ltd.

22801   Dd 291907   K26   9/77